THE DESERT CRIES

The Desert Cries

A Season of Flash Floods in a Dry Land

CRAIG CHILDS
Illustrations by Regan Choi

ARIZONA HIGHWAYS
BOOKS

Book Designer: MARY WINKELMAN VELGOS
Book Editor: BOB ALBANO
Copy Editor: EVELYN HOWELL

Publisher: WIN HOLDEN
Managing Editor: BOB ALBANO
Associate Editor: EVELYN HOWELL
Associate Editor: PK PERKIN McMAHON
Art Director: MARY WINKELMAN VELGOS
Photography Director: PETER ENSENBERGER
Production Director: CINDY MACKEY

Published by the Book Division of *Arizona Highways*® magazine, a monthly publication of the Arizona Department of Transportation, 2039 West Lewis Avenue, Phoenix, Arizona 85009.
Telephone: (602) 712-2200
Web site: www.arizonahighways.com

ARIZONA HIGHWAYS
BOOKS

FIRST PRINTING, 2002.
Printed in Singapore
Library of Congress Catalog Number 2001097637
ISBN 1-893860-64-7

CONTENTS

The Desert Cries *was written in memory of those who died in the five flash floods that are the subject of this book: Maria Socorro Ramirez Pedroza, Ruben Gavia Ramirez, Jose Eloy Olmedo Solis, Javier Castillo del Carmen, Juan Manuel Ortiz Hernandez, Lynn Anita Johnson, Chee Chin Yang, Elsa Pascual, Benjamin Partrick, Thierry Castell, Paul Lohr, Anitas Lohr, Sophie Froim, Beatrice Aline, Servane Allain, Charlotte Warmington, Anders Wassenius, Patty McCue Moran, and John Moran, and three others who were never identified.*

ACKNOWLEDGMENTS

This book stands entirely on the shoulders of other people. I extend my thanks to everyone who played a part, to the fire departments of Kingman and Douglas, to numerous rescuers in northern Arizona, to the city public works crew and police department of Douglas, and especially to John McHugh for a steadying voice in answering each of my questions. And of course, thank you, Nikki Welch Solper, pilot for the Arizona Department of Transportation, for flying me to nowhere and back.

AUTHOR'S NOTE

I was talking with a man who nearly died in a flash flood. He was telling me about a wall of water that had plunged down a narrow desert canyon in the Grand Canyon, striking him and two companions with no more than 15 seconds of warning. His companions, his sister and her husband, did not survive.

Of all of the details he revealed about the water, the violence, and the slim margin by which he escaped, what seemed most striking was that he had found peace while being dragged through the underside of this flood in the company of tumbling boulders and uprooted trees. During this ordeal, he let go of his life. He said that he found himself in a situation in which death would not be such a terrible thing. Only then did the flood release him.

I, too, have been taken down by a desert flash flood. Uncontrollable currents heavy with mud left my skin raw and bloodied. I look back at the floodwaters with only this question: How can peace and grace exist amid so much violence?

If you have never seen a flash flood, you will in this book, and you will meet survivors whose stories might help you understand such a paradox.

The Desert Cries tells the stories of five flash floods that killed 22 people on the Arizona deserts in August and September of 1997. I have gone to people and records to trace these events. Survivors willing to discuss circumstances divulged many small, but important, details. Other information came from journalists, eyewitnesses, gauging station reports, satellite images, and my own knowledge of the areas. I did not write these pieces to be read strictly as stories of disaster nor as cautionary tales. I wrote them to reveal a furious and elegant beast that few people ever get to see.

[prologue]

A STRANGE ATTRACTION

A thunderstorm warning comes on the television. Bold, red letters flash across the bottom of the screen. The kids are watching television. I don't know what show. My eyes are caught by the warning. Thunder booms outside.

I am in Prescott, Arizona, visiting the home of Walt Anderson, a renowned scientist and naturalist. He is my graduate school advisor, the one who reads my papers as I pursue a master's degree focusing on the dynamics of flash floods in American deserts. I have been compiling data from across Arizona, making field trips to measure terraces of flood debris, tracking storms on radar. I have chased the billowing heads of cumulus clouds across the state, driven like a lunatic along four-wheel-drive roads, sprinted thousands of feet down canyons with equipment banging on my back.

Seeing a flash flood catches God red-handed. A flood constitutes an act of such creation and destruction, of such raw energy, that you cannot avert your eyes. Some people travel the globe to witness solar eclipses or volcanic eruptions or the migration of millions of birds to a single waterway. They hope for the same thing I want when I chase floods — to accompany an event that is flawless, humbling, and eternal. Born in the dry country of central Arizona, my love is for water. The stroke of a desert flood across a once-dry floor enslaves my eyes.

When I was a child in the late 1970s, the swollen Salt River split Phoenix numerous times. I was astonished by the sudden destruction that water brought to this thirsty city. Bridges collapsed into torrents where there was usually no water at all. Lines of street lights fell over like old fence posts. Sidewalks broke open as if made of pie crust. I remember a light pole leaning from buckled concrete and shedding beams into the night at a skewed angle. I can name the years of great floods, recalling childhood and adulthood memories punctuated by moments of violence: death tolls and sand bags and helicopters sent to pluck desperate survivors from rock outcrops and treetops. Newspaper headlines were anxious to blame somebody — a government agency, a guide for an outdoors company, foolish motorists, bridge builders — anybody but the desert and the rain.

In the house where Walt and I are trying to carry on a conversation, my body is rigid. My eyes snap over to the television now and then. Reports coming in. Dangerous thunderstorms across northwestern Arizona: Yavapai County, Mohave County, Coconino County. Flash flood warnings.

Walt knows that my mind is far from here. "Do you want to go?" he finally asks.

I turn to face him from the television. "Yes," I say.

He looks seriously at me, studying my eyes. "I'll drive."

We take the north road toward the Granite Mountain Wilderness. Rain comes in throbs, turning the windshield white. The wipers slop waves of water back and forth, clearing just enough so that we can see the road, covered by mist from exploding rain. Through the side window I

see a sheet of water flow over the ground, not in a wash or a drainage, but right out in the open, unashamed. The road drops toward Skull Valley Wash. We will find our flood there.

Several months earlier Walt and I went out to the Sonoran Desert to survey the remnants of a massive flood. The place resembled the scene of an invasion left eerily silent. We found saguaro cacti standing in the open desert 30 feet from the nearest wash with tangles of flood debris caught high in their sharp spines. We found boulders trapped in the arms of mesquite trees. Force and suddenness were written everywhere.

I had been doing research in the burnt deserts along the Mexican border, in central Arizona washes, and in the wilderness abyss of the Grand Canyon in northern Arizona. I took on this field project because it fascinated me that the driest parts of the world, where annual precipitation sometimes amounts to only a couple of inches, could suddenly become the focus of so much water. The flood water always appears fickle, as if the irony of drought and storm create an outlandish language. An insignificant, dry canyon can suddenly burst with more water volume than the Colorado River.

In the western Grand Canyon I measured the speeds and heights of flood bores — the fresh, leading edges of these flash floods. Waves of foam and tree parts, red with sandstone or brown with mud, caromed into the canyons, howling with speed. However, some just crept their way through, building slowly over an hour or two.

The swift floods often catch hikers by surprise. Water rumbles out of a distant canyon while the skies over hikers' heads are perfectly clear. The slow floods find vehicles crossing washes, snare them, and grow until the vehicles capsize, and mud and sand consumes them. For each foot the flood rises up the side of a car, 1,500 pounds of water are displaced, in essence making the car 1,500 pounds lighter. Cars are often carried away in only 2 feet of water, sometimes with occupants still clinging to the steering wheels or the roofs.

When I searched the literature, I found little direct information on flash floods themselves. Most research focused on the aftermath with measurements and postulations concerning what might have happened. In deserts, flash floods are unpredictable, short lived, and often occur in remote locations. Thus, they are hard to find and research.

The desert is not as bare as most nondesert dwellers think, but it certainly has less plant cover than much of the world. This vegetative void allows rain to strike directly against the earth. When it does, especially during the thunderstorms of summer and autumn, 2 or 3 inches of rain can fall in six minutes. Most of a year's precipitation might fall in only one afternoon.

Water gathers, channeled by the landscape. Torrents run into washes, arroyos, and canyons, sucking and gasping as the flow grabs pieces of earth and tears them free. The flood grows, irrepressibly looking for the way down. That sequence defines the desert, the place at the bottom, where the water gathers.

The best research material I found originated in Israel, where flood patterns of the Negev Desert are similar to those of Arizona. An Israeli team, tracking a flash flood, had to scramble to pull equipment out before

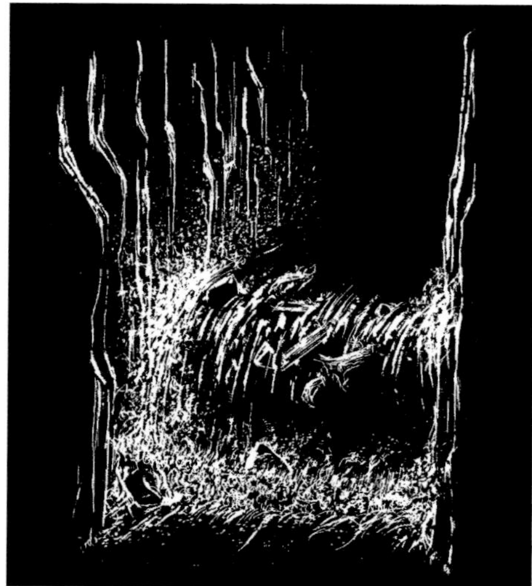

it was crushed by the rising turbulence and debris. I found that accounts of most first-hand research on floods are decorated with complaints of injuries or damaged gear or the frustration of having to evacuate before adequate data could be gathered.

In the Grand Canyon I placed simple markers in a flood's way and stood by with a stopwatch. Then I ran downstream, barely ahead of the flood, to place more markers and time the growling advance of water and wreckage. I finally had to get out of the way when the flow blew my markers end over end.

My data agreed with that from Israel. We both found that the bulk of the flood actually moves faster than the leading wave that it pushes. The point is counterintuitive, but incontestable. The flood constantly overtakes its front, stacking up until it becomes a rolling wall constantly gaining height. Like an anxious child, the flow pushes to clear a path so it can pick up speed. Faster and faster. Higher and higher.

Driving down the west side of the Bradshaw Mountains, Walt and I follow the road into the Sonoran Desert. When Skull Valley Wash, fixed in place by the walls of a slight canyon, first comes into view, we see the flood below us, its turbulent coils and vortices overtaking each other.

I urge Walt to drive faster. After a couple of miles, we forge ahead of the flood. We pull off the road. Drawing tight the hoods of our raincoats, we walk to the edge of the roadcut and look down, bending forward to keep the rain out of our faces. There is no movement in the floor, only sand pocked by rain.

After less than a minute, a fist of water comes through. Moving fast, it strikes boulders in the way, deluging them. Within a few seconds, the floor is filled with roiling water. I didn't bring any tools for measurement. I only have a notebook with me.

My eyes freeze on the movement below me. The flood is unstoppable, but not careless. It makes courtly moves, whirlpools starting up, then quickly washing out when they are no longer needed. It displays discernment and intelligence, but not like our own. It is a different kind of animal, one that plays by an imperishable set of rules. This is what I so much appreciate about floods, that they cannot be possessed or commanded.

I sometimes capture flood water in specimen vials, storing it so that the sediment would drift to the bottom. When I open the vials to measure sediment concentration, what strikes me is that the speed and immediacy are vanished. I have inert water in a glass. I've captured no flood.

I turn to Walt. "Let's get downstream. There's a good bridge, right?"

"Yes," he says.

"Let's see it from there."

When we reach the bridge, a number of floods have already entered from other drainages. Standing waves of mud and water pour through,

filling a broad wash. A cow stands on the shore, its hooves mired in mud. If it doesn't get out of there soon, the water will take it. We park on one side and walk out to the middle of the bridge. The flood sweeps below us, hissing with sand. The rain is gone. The storm has already roamed away to the north.

Slabs of construction timber and the splintered remains of a dead cottonwood tree sail down. As they hit the bridge abutments, there is a deep sound, like a struck timpani. The bridge thumps back, jarring for a second. Then the raft of wood moves on.

Floods can carry remarkable loads of sediment: boulders, trees, cars, and sand. Because of the desert's dry nature, sediment doesn't often get moved. Boulders tumble from a cliff face and pile up. Trees die and topple. When a flood runs, it gathers and carries everything it can find like a fervent garbage collector cleaning the streets. With the added force of all of this debris it has gathered, the flood becomes a sand blaster, taking out the live trees and tearing at the cliff walls. Sometimes desert floods are only 10 percent water. The other 90 percent is a slurry of earth. Fifty-ton boulders have been recorded on the move in Arizona floods, carried for miles.

Look at high mountain streams. They usually are clear because they run constantly, preening and cleaning themselves of excess debris, as meticulous as a cat. Desert floods, on the other hand, carry the weight of the earth like an animal gone mad.

I look at Walt. The wash here is wide. If there were a constriction somewhere, a canyon, then the turbulence would lift to an unbearable level. I want to hear the bellow of water and feel mist washing my face. I ask him, "Is there a constriction downstream of here, a canyon or anything?"

"There's a place about 15 miles away," he says.

"Let's go."

Fifteen miles later we are standing in the sun. I pace across dry sand where the wash closes into somewhat of a canyon. I look upstream. No flood. We wait. It never even rained here, and the air is hot. I trace shapes in the sand with the tips of my boots. There is not even a breeze.

"I don't know," I say. "It should be here any minute."

The minutes go on without a flood. Finally, I look to Walt and say, sheepishly, "I got greedy."

He nods his head.

"The flood must have died out somewhere," I say. "It probably spread across the sand and disappeared. All of that water just sank into the ground without enough power to move it this far down."

We return to his vehicle, get in, and open a map between us. We agree on another drainage that should have caught some of the storm. "It should have something, right?" I ask.

"Sure," he answers.

I have a friend who lives in the canyon desert of Moab, Utah. At midnight during a summer storm, he woke to the sound of rain tormenting the roof of his home. He put on his clothes and a raincoat and walked to the nearest drainage, a place called Mill Creek that runs through the middle of town. His hood pulled over his head, he arrived at the overpass for the main street to see, in the faint luminescence of a nearby streetlight, another person standing down near the creek.

Then a third person with his face obscured beneath a hood walked by and said quietly, "Here to see the flood?"

My friend nodded in return.

The man stopped a polite distance away to stare into the drainage. Within half an hour the flood came.

It is perhaps the fierceness or the unrelenting show of force that draws people to floods. Imagine seeing a flood. Imagine what it would do to your heart. Have you ever stood next to a train going at top speed, stood so close you had to squint for the wind and the steel passing too fast to watch? Imagine being there as it derails.

Do you see why I go?

Walt and I drive east again in search of this thing and park near a barbed wire fence. Climbing over the fence, we enter another sand wash and follow it up into a canyon. Saguaro cacti line the slopes of the wash, trailing off into the desert. After walking for about a mile, we stop. On the canyon floor, a thin band of water wraps like a rope between rocks. It noses its way toward us, no more than 5 inches wide. Its front is a frothing miniature shield of red foam. I've seen flood foam before, churning barricades of it 5 feet tall tossed into the air from wave crests and behind boulders. Walt and I both crouch and stick our fingers into this tiny flood. Foam adheres to our knuckles.

He smiles. "It's kind of cute."

For the next hour we walk astride this newborn trickle, following its slow turns. The flow takes 10 minutes to fill a hole, then rises out of it to

continue downstream. We guess at what it might do next, its choice of courses. Will it sneak behind a rock, or will it pass under the arch of a fallen mesquite branch? Watching the water is like watching an animal's most candid manners.

For years I had been trying to map floods, trying to predict the impact of different storms in different regions. Flood deaths are too common in the Southwest's deserts. Usually, the people killed are caught by surprise, having no idea that the desert could do such a thing. Boy Scouts have rappelled into canyons, dropping blindly, and directly, into seething floodwaters. Vehicles have been struck head-on, windshields bursting on impact. I hunted the academic libraries and the wilderness canyons, seeking patterns and reasons. What I found about floods was a scramble of information that did not come easily to order.

Over all of my field work, a shadow casts a pall. In just more than a month, 22 people died in flash floods within the boundaries of my research. During the floods that I personally witnessed and recorded, it was difficult to shrug off the weight of this loss.

The day I began my research on flash floods in 1997, spending the morning getting my notes together and filling out papers, eight people were killed in a border flood between Arizona and Mexico. A couple of days later, a passenger train derailed because of a flash flood in Arizona's western desert.

Events piled up quickly, as they do each year from July to September when the floods come the hardest. I studied the forensic reports on some of those who died in hopes of understanding the forces that had taken them under and stripped them of their clothes, their jewelry, and their lives.

Also, many people lived.

I repeated their tribulations and close calls to see if there was any key to understanding hidden there. There are no ordinary answers I can give about floods. All that I could find was that desert floods, with their peculiar combination of sublimity and horror, are far greater than the frailty of our bodies. They obey laws that we often think do not apply to us. We build our bridges and our hiking trails and our railroads arrogantly. We migrate from other states, moving to a land we accuse of being eternally parched. We forget the rule of the desert, that the floods will come, and rarely when we are ready.

The water that Walt and I follow is whimsical and incalculable. This small amount behaves with remarkable personality, picking up and abandoning sticks, curiously fingering into holes before moving on.

It should have been a raging flood, or it should have been nothing at all.

Instead it is a quixotic little stream. It is the same water that has killed so many people; the water that is rich with nutrients replenishing the desert; the water that sinks into the sand and fills the deep aquifers.

I squat and stick my finger into the gentle flow. I pull it out and taste it as if I've just poked into fresh cake batter. The water tastes of salty, astringent minerals. It tastes like tears.

DOUGLAS, SOUTHEASTERN ARIZONA

A hard-backed row of peaks rises 1,200 feet over the desert northeast of Douglas near the Mexican border. These mountains are named Perilla, a Spanish word referring to an ear lobe, a crested shape of desert anatomy. Fissured cliffs of the Perillas lean slightly to the east, and below them runs a deft web of natural drainages called washes or arroyos.

The drainages cut into the desert's smooth ground, coalescing into larger and larger arroyos like threads drawn together by a hand. A waist-high forest of creosote bush dominates the vegetation. Gangly arms of ocotillo grow in isolated stands.

This is the Chihuahuan Desert, a dry territory of hot summers and freezing winters, a marginal place to run cattle and no good for growing crops.

Each dirt road out here has been remade numerous times after being eaten away by flash floods that gushed over the sides of arroyos. The progress of erosion can actually be seen, marked by each time that the roads have had to be constructed farther from the arroyos, keeping one step ahead of the undermining floods that come down the drainages.

These usually dry strings of waterways lead west toward the town of Douglas, a small border town where Spanish and English are equally mixed into conversations. A Main Street sort of place, Douglas has a good number of auto mechanics and diners specializing in pork chops and enchiladas drowning in red chile sauce. The economy hereabouts has never been especially good nor entirely disastrous. The town seems outdated in the world, like a place that will soon die off but keeps sputtering along. Chances are, Douglas will outlive every fad and every metropolis, sitting patiently in the desert, withstanding the wind and the drought and, occasionally, the flood.

When the waterways reach the outskirts of town, they turn from sandy washes into hard-packed dirt roads, then into paved streets. Arrays of boulevards funnel toward the middle of town. This alignment favors a flood, which grows until it finds some center point and sends all its force into one place. This place, in Douglas, is where a flood did find its first people.

Near the town's center, where streets run into each other like dry intersecting rivers, nine of us stand around a sealed manhole cover near Ninth Street and F Avenue. A gathering of police detectives, firefighters, city workers, a photographer, and myself, we are here because this is where floods from the desert washes converge in an underground network engineered to take the water away, like it is something wild that the town can't afford to have running loose in the neighborhoods. The corner stoplight turns red and then green, maintaining an orderly flow of traffic. One of the firefighters signals cars to go around us. Sidewalks are busy.

Frank Garcia, a hazardous materials technician, lowers a tube through one of the silver-dollar-sized holes in the manhole cover. He checks his equipment, looking for oxygen content and methane fumes in the storm drain that runs beneath F Avenue.

"It's clear," he says.

One of the city workers kneels on the cover and pounds around the seal with a heavy-duty screwdriver. Then he jams a crowbar into a space between the asphalt and the iron. After a few lunges with his body, he peels the cover off the street. The disk rolls back, landing to the side with a loud, solid crash. A gasp of cool air pushes out. The underworld is open. I think: This is where they had been; this is where they struggled for their lives.

We all gather around the hole, looking into a black pit 12 feet deep and 2 feet wide. The firefighters here once searched the darkness and debris below us for bodies. Detectives spoke with the survivors. City maintenance workers dealt with the aftermath.

We shine flashlights into this place. Cramped and humid, the hole leads into the strange underworld of storm drains. It is not a place for people. That is what strikes me first. It is a place for water. I imagine the fear that must have filled this place, the howling voices of people in the rumble of water.

The photographer, a woman with long, dark hair, is also an artist, here to render images of the site. She scans the faces around her. Nobody else is making a move.

"I'll go first," she says. She turns and crawls into the hole, descending a ladder cemented into the curved wall. Heads move in closer to watch her descent. She calls up to let us know the air is cold and smells musty. But not bad. A flash of light bursts from the hole as she takes a photograph of our circle of heads.

I follow her, strapping on a headlamp and climbing down the ladder. The air smells dank, rich with water and decay. At the end of the ladder I jump the last couple of feet, landing firmly in a shallow pool of water. A cramped tunnel runs north and south from here. In both directions the tunnel disappears at infinity, coming to a dark, obscure pinpoint in the distance. I crouch. I can see the photographer 10 feet ahead, her body hunched down. She looks like she is tumbling down a windpipe. She tells me not to move. There is a blue flash of light. She arranges her camera gear and shuffles farther ahead.

"This is really intense," she calls to me. "If a flood came down here, you couldn't hold onto anything. It wouldn't take much water at all."

I touch the curve of concrete with my right palm and my fingers. The tunnel system is designed to move water so efficiently that it sucks the streets dry during a rain. There is no error down here, just the expert and indifferent industry of a storm drain.

"Yes," I say quietly. "Hardly any water at all."

My headlamp swings north, then south. The tunnel stretches into infinity, eating the light. I look up and see a ring of faces staring down. No one else wants to come. They decline my invitation. They are here only to help should we need it.

I move into the constraining passageway, opposite the direction taken by the photographer. My shoulders take up the space, and my boots scratch through gravel, water, and soaked leaves. Pieces of garbage are mixed in. I pull out a tape measure and run it from side to side — 3 1/2 feet in diameter, not at all the size for a human. My body strains to find the right posture. I move farther into the tunnel, pulling out my notebook to record the size and distribution of gravel and rocks and sand. I am curious about what is down here, what kind of debris remains after strong water comes through.

The photographer, 20 feet behind me, tells me to stop. I turn my headlight toward her so that she can fix her lens on me in the darkness. When I turn back around, she flashes a picture. The shadow of my tucked body shoots straight down the passageway. The instant black image of me streaks away for just a 30th of a second, stretched out for blocks. Then darkness takes over again. The light of my headlamp seems insignificant. I follow it.

The photographer is much farther behind me, the flash of her camera now just a tap of distant light. Claustrophobia is so close at hand that I can hear it feeding on my fears. There is an illusion that the tunnel bends. It hurts my eyes to try and straighten it out.

I write down everything that I find. The plastic wrapper from a burrito, its ingredients listed in Spanish. Pieces of metal, small car parts. There are willow and poplar leaves, scales of junipers — all ornamental lawn plants from around Douglas.

I also find some shredded bits of soaptree yucca and branches of

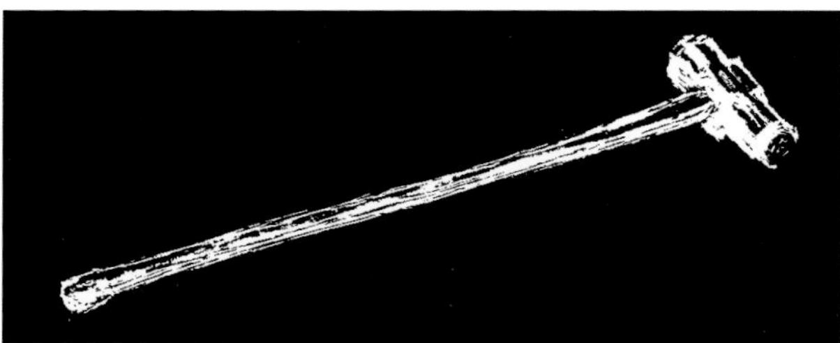

creosote bush. That tells me that the water originally comes from outside of town, from the desert.

The next thing I find is a sledgehammer. It couldn't have gotten into the storm drain on its own. Metal grates over the openings that let water from the street pour into the tunnel would have caught it. The hammer is not store-bought new. In fact, it looks like it has been down here for a few years. The illegal immigrants who work their way from Mexico into the United States through this tunnel depend on such tools to loosen the manhole covers to get out of the tunnels. After using the tools, the immigrants leave them for the next people to come through.

I lift the tool free from the wet, packed sand. The wood of the handle is deeply worn, like driftwood. The iron head is pocked by hungry rust.

I turn toward the photographer and shout that I have found a sledgehammer. My words twist along the crawlway, half-echoing, half-dampening, becoming something other than my voice. She can't hear me. I am alone. I wipe sand off the handle and hold it in two fists.

When I look for the photographer, I can't see her at all. I set down the sledgehammer. I reach up and turn off my headlamp. The only thing

I see is a distant crescent of light from below the open manhole. It looks as if it were miles away.

Otherwise, it is so dark that I cannot feel the smallness of this enclosure. I could be planted in space, staring at a bright, moon-like sliver.

If I panicked, I would run. If I tried to run, my back would involuntarily straighten, and I would scrape my head like a brake pad across the concrete curve above me and wedge myself into the tunnel.

That is why I am frightened to crouch in the dark of this tunnel. It is made for water, not for people.

AUGUST 6

Anxious, but wearing the steady gaze of commuters, several dozen people gather at the Hotel Yolanda in Agua Prieta, Mexico, across the border from Douglas, Arizona.

It is nearing midnight.

The people mill around the stairs and watch the rain through huge floor-to-ceiling pane windows. The rain is growing to the north. The storm curls inward and throws lightning, dropping water across the Chihuahuan Desert and onto the Perilla Mountains.

The waiting people don't know about the storm in the mountains or the web of drainages that lead to Douglas's storm sewers. They anxiously await the final leg of a long and dangerous journey. The rain adds to the sense of foreboding that they brought with them. They hold their baggage close, satchels and bags with their most needed and cherished belongings. Some carry papers with them, documentation of their origins, their family names. They are ready to go.

The smuggler examines them. Well paid, he's the man these people call coyote. *The coyote exudes an air of consequence and gruff superiority. He does not ask questions nor invite discussion. He has made sure that the travelers know there are unseen dangers ahead of them in the United States, dangers that he tells them only he can ward off. He selects 13 to come with him under the cover of darkness and rain.*

Most of these 13 migrants traveled here from no closer than 900 miles to the south, in the tropics: a 34-year-old woman from Mexico City; two men between 18 and 22; two southern Mexican women, one with her 2-year-old daughter balanced on her hip; one man from Guanajuato on his way to see family in Chicago; an 18-year-old man from Michoacan; and five others, origins unspoken.

The rest will have to wait. Why these 13 are chosen — personal histories, physical statures, a certain composure to their faces — remains the coyote's business alone.

These illegal migrants are not traveling for a promised land or for starved dreams of riches. All they expect across the border is a series of menial jobs: hard, stooped labor of crop work, replanting forests in clear-cut sites in the Northwest, cleaning houses, waiting in urban migrant camps to be called out for a job, or picking heavy watermelons, and tossing them to coworkers on a moving truck.

Few United States citizens will take such jobs, so the labor comes from the south. It comes from people who learn to outmaneuver the meticulous trackers of la Migra, *the United States Border Patrol; people who leave close families and communities to cross the desert; people who pay a coyote to quietly deposit them on the other side of the border.*

A steady rain wets their shoulders as they walk north from the Hotel Yolanda for a couple of blocks. The weather is not hard and fierce, the kind that yields floods and sends people running to shelter.

However, 15 miles to the northeast, over the Perilla Mountains, the weather wears a different face. The rain up there is the kind that comes so hard that people wake up, their eyes darting around as if there is sudden danger.

The Perilla Mountains stand with mouths open, drawing the water down into the arroyos that lead toward Douglas.

It is now half past midnight, and the rain is beginning to pick up at the border.

The 13 travelers are now led into a deep drainage ditch running parallel along the border at Douglas's International Avenue. In three hours they are to meet their second contact at a manhole cover in town. He will transport them farther into the country.

Each had paid around $1,400 for this service, some of them sacrificing 10 or 15 years of savings in Mexico to cover the cost of safe passage, for the border is a terrifying place, a land of opportunists. Gang members sometimes come down from Phoenix, armed for violence because they have heard of easy prey coming across. On the Mexican side, young men wearing scarves over their faces assail migrants with baseball bats, a brutal extortion ensuring the need for hired protection. Even the coyotes are known to set upon their own clients, sometimes sexually attacking women who come without men.

The band of 13 meets a second coyote who, with the first one, leads the way to the edge of the deeply cut arroyo that runs along the border. The arroyo's walls are heavily eroded, 20 feet tall, blocking the view of anyone above. One coyote waves his hand, sending a message to young men and boys farther west along the border. Decoys, they dart into the wash and scramble up the bank on the United States side, running just within view of Border Patrol agents. Spotlights on top of towers flash against them. There is shouting. Maybe the decoys will be caught and sent back, or maybe they will be able to sprint back into Mexico before a hand can touch them, as if it is a game of tag. This choreography happens every night.

With the attention of the Border Patrol diverted, the 13 travelers and two coyotes descend into the arroyo with practiced acrobatics. Each person scrambles down a short length of nylon rope hand over hand. Everything moves swiftly, each person sliding down the last few feet of the muddy bank. The child is passed gently from hand to hand as the coyote in front hisses rapidly between his teeth to get his followers to move faster.

The child's mother reaches up and grabs her little girl, wrapped in a blanket, her small face covered against the rain. Two years earlier, the then-pregnant mother was caught crossing in the same place and sent back. She managed to gather the money needed again.

A tangle of natural objects — grass, branches, cactus pieces, rocks — and human rubbish — tires, oil bottles, plastic wrappers, newspapers — mat the arroyo's floor, strapped and woven together by past floodwaters.

The migrants follow the sculpted course of sand until coming to the southern end of a storm drain tunnel below F Avenue in the town of Douglas. A few of them have flashlights. They turn them on and crouch in the passageway, a low, concrete tunnel half-clogged with mud and old flash flood material. Only 2½ feet of space remains above the mud at the tunnel's mouth.

The second coyote tells them that they must move quickly into the hole. He explains that if they keep track of overhead shafts that lead to manholes, they will pass nine of them. At the 10th shaft, 10 blocks from here, they need to climb up a ladder built into the shaft and through a manhole to the street. A tool will be waiting for them on the ladder so they can pry the cover open.

The next contact will watch for them from the surface. One of the migrants objects to the coyotes not leading them any farther. He says that he expected to be escorted all the way, not dropped off at a hole in the ground. And how can they be guaranteed that the next contact will be there? And this tool? What if it is not there? The second coyote says that there is no time to argue. He demands that they go now, before the diversion fails.

Crouching so low that their knees knock into their chests, the travelers half crawl into the F Avenue storm drain. Their lights vanish into the rounding distance. A small stream is flowing, only a few inches deep. The two coyotes turn back quickly and sprint toward Mexico.

With backs scraping along the smooth, curved ceiling, the migrants push their way along, stopping to shine a light against the first manhole.

It is 12½ feet up a narrow, round shaft ribbed with ladder rungs. They say nothing and continue toward the 10th ladder.

Rain outside beats a cadence, like gravel pouring onto pavement. They can hear it steadily increase, but they cannot see the storm's path and intensity.

Thin streams of water coming down from the street turns the tunnel into an endless echo chamber. The sound of water is all around, but it does not sound dangerous. It only sounds like the underbelly of a town, the drips and gurgles of drainage.

It is now 12:45 A.M., barely an hour since the group left the hotel.

Across the Perilla Mountains northeast of Douglas, the clouds have broken, having yielded most of their rain. An inch has fallen in the last half hour, creating an enormous runoff. Creosote bushes and ocotillo plants cannot stanch the water's flow. Dozens of minor washes carry water from the mountains across the desert toward Douglas. The washes deliver the load to dirt roads, which turn into paved roads.

Water sheets over sidewalks and lawns, taking street after street with single-minded momentum. At each intersection, portions of the water steal down into street gutters. The metal gutter grates drown under debris and water.

The water takes maybe 15 minutes to come to full force and sprint into Douglas.

It is now 1 A.M.

The pilgrimage of migrants reaches the underside of Ninth Street and F Avenue. They have passed nine overhead shafts with ladders leading to the street. One more block and they will reach their destination.

From ahead comes a hollow sound like wind passing through a glass tube. Flashlight beams lift as the migrants look toward the sound. People shuffle into each other, stopping, peering beyond the line of shoulders. They see nothing, but the sound grows into a howl. They are uncertain of what they are hearing. The howl becomes a roar. At that instant, they know. It is water.

The man in front, the one who had argued with the coyotes, turns quickly, casting his light up the ladder to Ninth Street. He shouts to the woman behind him, grabbing her shoulder to help her up.

The sound becomes unbearable. It growls and screams as it bears down on the migrants. The second woman hands her 2-year-old to the man as she hurries up the ladder. She throws an arm toward her daughter, but just as she grabs for the girl, the water hits.

It smashes into the man like he's the bowsprit of a ship. He loses his flashlight as he keels over and rolls head-first with the girl in his hands. In darkness, bodies pile into each other, as water overtakes them. Shouts, screams. Arms and legs tangling. They try to wedge themselves against the roundness of the tunnel.

The man who was in the lead is upside-down, his head pushed into his chest, the girl still crammed into his arms. He doesn't know up from down and can't find the air. His body uncoils in a panic, his arms flailing. The girl slips away.

When he rights himself, he shouts for the girl. His voice goes nowhere. He pushes his back like a shield against the water. It charges over his shoulders into his face. There is no light. Just sound and force.

Two men behind him field the toddler. They pass and shove the small body ahead, toward the ladder.

In the turmoil, hands fumble. Again the water takes the child, sweeping her past a couple of people before someone catches her by her wrist. The men call to each other and push her ahead again. Hands reach to hands. The child, helpless and blind, feels a grip around her thigh, two hands snatching her under her arms. Finally, the man in front who had braced his arms against the tunnel, grabs her and passes her up to her mother on the ladder.

Without his arms braced against the tunnel, the man loses his balance. His fingers drag across the arched ceiling of the tunnel. Other people clog against his feet, and they tumble away in a single mass. He races downstream. A block farther, he tries to grab the next ladder, but his fingers just snap past the shaft, too fast. By the third block, he is traveling so fast that he has no sense of direction. He feels bones break in his hand when it reaches for the ladder. In the rush of his adrenaline and heroism, turned upside-down and unable to breathe, he feels the fear. Now he knows that he will die.

The two women climb to the Ninth Street manhole cover. The woman at the top finds a metal tool hanging from the highest rung. She snatches it and beats against the iron cover. Terrified voices speed down the storm drain below her, becoming more distant. Their unnerving wails turn to echoes, blurring into the water. Finally, the cries are gone. Water gulps and slaps below the manhole chute. It seals them in. She can hear it rising, and she pounds harder.

The woman below pulls her little girl up into her shoulder, tucking her safely as the water comes around her feet. She climbs one more rung until she is pressed against the woman above her. The water reaches her knees, then her waist.

The woman atop the ladder takes the edge of the metal tool and works around the seal of the manhole, trying to be calm, to think.

Three blocks downstream, a woman hangs alone onto the third rung of a manhole ladder, her legs sucked into the water below her. She lugs herself from one rung to the next. Finally against the manhole, she pushes with one hand, then with two. There is no movement. The cover is jammed. She pounds and screams. Her call carries to surrounding buildings.

A woman who lives along F Avenue wakes up. She turns back her bed covers and walks to her front door. She opens it. Up and down the block she sees no one, just a town glistening from a heavy rain gone by. Yet she knows she hears a voice, desperate but far away and impossible to locate. She grabs a raincoat and walks into the wet street where garbage and desert debris are scattered. The gutters are clogged. There is no one; no screams, no shouting. She notices that the storm drain must be full. The four vent holes in the manhole cover are spewing water. The woman goes back into her home.

Another block downstream from there, two men were able to climb a ladder before the water took them. They shove with their backs against the manhole, listening to the voices speed away below them. One still has a flashlight. They use it to study the manhole, looking for purchase for their fingers. It does not budge. They believe a car must be parked on top. They throw their weight against it, but it is hard to find leverage from this position. The water sweeps up to their chests. Then it gives them only a few last inches of breathing room. They hang onto the ladder and each other, waiting for the water to swallow them. They turn their heads up so that their lips touch the manhole, desperately breathing the final bits of air.

Meanwhile, water swirls around the two women's collarbones as they cling to the ladder at Ninth Street.

The mother uses her back to lift, holding the girl against her own throat. Ribs lining the underside of the cover cut into her back. The second woman pounds at the seal with her tool. The cover finally gives way. Night air rushes in on them. The heavy iron saucer rolls back and falls soundly against the pavement. The sky opens. Stars.

The child will have nightmares from this memory. She will not

forget the yelling and the deaths of strangers. Grasping the sensations but not the reasons, she will remember the smell of mud and the force of flood wind. She will remember the coyote's face, the sound of water approaching in a black enclosure, the hands of men who saved her, the one who slipped loose from below the ladder and vanished.

Across the corner from a mortuary and an auto repair shop, the two women climb from the hole to the quiet street. The air is middle-of-the-night calm, the town still. After replacing the cover, they skirt from streetlights into darkness, the child tucked like a fragile and precious belonging.

The two men downstream have given up on their manhole cover. It will not move. Their bodies compress together as they breathe the last air. They wait for the water to consume the entire passageway, but it does not. It begins to drop. Slowly, it winds down toward the tunnel below them. Finally, when it is low enough, they drop into the tunnel that runs under F Avenue. Swimming through mud where the fallen are now buried, they return to the point where they had entered the storm drain. Crawling out of chest-deep debris into the drainage ditch that runs along the border, they scramble away into the night.

The port of entry on Pan American Avenue sits over a point where the drainage ditch flows into a covered culvert, which is capped by a steel grate. Around 1:30 A.M., city workers arrive to clear debris that is causing the ditch to overflow, flooding businesses in a nearby shopping center. Frank Amarillas, the port director, unlocks a gate for the backhoe, then walks to the debris pile to watch the excavation work. As the backhoe makes a sweep, Amarillas spies a bundle. A bag of marijuana, he thinks, reaching down. It would not be an uncommon find along the border. As he tugs at it he finds that, instead, it is a woman's body.

The search turns up children's clothing and toys and then a duffel with personal belongings and papers describing a woman in her mid-30s from Mexico's Colima state.

At 6 A.M., searchers find a second body. It is the man who had flung the two women and the child up the ladder in the storm drain, the one

who had argued with the coyotes. The body is encased in mud.

After sunrise, another body is found, and more personal papers are disentombed.

In the afternoon, both sides of the border crowd with onlookers, all of them sweating out this 100-plus-degree day to voice astonishment. On the Mexican side, a woman with a child hoisted on one hip, another child holding her hand, is heard saying, "Oh my god, how could they do that — cross in that storm?"

A young boy sits in the heat, out of shouting distance from the crowd and the searchers. He is playing a game, throwing rocks into the mud-filled arroyo. His target is a wad of fabric and debris. A man walks over and asks what he is doing. The boy describes the game. The man looks closer and tells the boy to stop immediately. He nervously calls searchers over. The fabric is a piece of clothing. Under it are three bodies piled one on top of the next. Six people are dead; five have escaped. The search continues for two other bodies.

Even with cadaver-searching dogs and block-by-block hunts through the debris-filled tunnel, searchers from the police and fire department ultimately must surrender.

The relatives of a missing man, both in Mexico and in the United States, are caught in grief. They make phone calls to officials. They come to Douglas. They demand that the search continue. This tragedy should not have happened, they exclaim.

These migrants, the relatives say, were workers that the United States needed. The United States owes it to the families to at least produce the body, and many of the searchers agree, digging harder. But he cannot be found. Rescuers are sickened and exhausted.

A phone call comes from Chicago. Another family has not heard from a young man who was supposed to be heading to Chicago. He was not a citizen of the United States and was supposed to be crossing in Douglas. Searchers fear that two are now missing.

Anger is directed toward the coyotes. Families and officials call for them to reveal themselves. They want to know why the coyotes chose not to escort the migrants all the way through this rainstorm, why they did not warn them about floods. And where was the next contact who could have loosened the manhole covers?

No one turns the coyotes in, nor do they surrender.

Smugglers working back at the Hotel Yolanda shrug the incident off. It's a risk of the game, they say.

Twelve days later, a flood again spills from thunderheads in the Perillas. As if in a gesture of ownership, the flood washes two bodies free.

MOJAVE DESERT, WESTERN ARIZONA

In the jump seat of a small plane I sit directly behind the pilot and copilot. My face hovers at the window, then I lean across and look out the other window. I reach forward and tap the pilot on the shoulder and with a finger indicate a circling motion. The engines are loud, covering any words I might use. She nods to me and banks the plane, so one wing points down and the other up. Now I can see straight down into the heart of a ragged, isolated mountain range. It looks like a nest of dark dragons.

What pleases me most in my life is to see raw and rugged land like this. Even if I cannot touch it, if the land races a thousand feet beneath me, I am enlivened to merely witness it. In the headlong madness of our civilization, we need something older and wiser than ourselves left untouched. We need natural things that have not been imprinted with the endless mark of humanity and that are left absent of highways and houses and towns. I have become a student of landforms because of this pleasure in wild lands and my curiosity about the shapes and patterns found there. I want to know how a flash flood will carve the desert, why rocks and mountains are shaped the way that they are. I study the way drainages interact, and how they focus flash floods.

The plane belongs to the Arizona Department of Transportation. It is prop-driven, its wings mounted above the fuselage so that the view of the ground is not blocked. On this flight across western Arizona, we are passing over the Sonoran and Mojave deserts, surveying the lay of flash flood drainages that cut into the parched mountains.

In the few places where we see railroad tracks or paved roads, it is strikingly clear how they clip across subtle flood drainages on the desert floor. These slight depressions likely are unbeknown to the engineers who did the planning and to automobile drivers who are hit by spasms of water during a storm. Sometimes it helps to step back — or up in this case — and get a better perspective. My view from the air makes the

flood courses entirely visible. The plane circles twice as I scribble in my ratty field notebook, then I tap the pilot's shoulder again to let her know we can move on.

The mountains below are studded with fins and sharp spines. There is no sign of humanity, no place for dirt roads or buildings. In fact, I have the impression that a human would be swallowed up just by trying to walk around down there. The jumbled topography goes on for nearly a hundred miles with crooks and stabs reaching up for the plane. Yet there is a constant glimmer of sensuality secluded deep within each range. Floods have left hundreds of wandering canyons that slice like sinuous ribbons into the ground. From up here, the canyons look elaborate, richly decorating the senseless chaos of stone. The mountains are male, the canyons female. And the floods are rare and genderless.

From there we pass east out of the dry mountains over a desert that stretches taut as a drum head. The land becomes a smooth absolution, cleared of all ruts and ridges. Still, the mark of water endures. Instead of canyons, a luscious circuitry of washes stretches over the land. The washes wind and coalesce and come apart. They look alive, even though they are absolutely dry. I tap the pilot's shoulder. She takes us into a steep circle. I stare down into a wash of white sand, and my finger touches the window. I trace the wash's path.

Looking across the desert from an airplane, many people might see vast regions of bitterness and desolation. I see a landscape of hope. It isn't from some kind of cheerful optimism that I see this. I have spent enough time on the ground to know the difference between Pollyannaism and reality. What I see even in dryness is water running across this place, leaving ornate marks of its passage in the form of canyons and washes or arroyos. Natural processes are recorded unconditionally. The virulence and duplicity I sometimes see in humanity, the lies and underhandedness, are not registered here on the land. That is why I see hope.

We fly to the southeast, toward the city of Kingman, Arizona. Calling it a city is a technicality. It is not much larger than Douglas, sort of a sister city in the Mojave Desert, a place east of the Colorado River, far enough east that it is not a river town at all. We have already been out for a couple of hours, and I have been studying canyons and washes from the plane since just about the Mexican border, 200 miles south of here. I have been unfolding maps across my lap, taking notes on the topography and the impact of water left on the mostly bare ground below. The irony is that each of these waterways will carry water for maybe only a few hours of each year, or perhaps not a drop for years on end.

We fly over a place called Red Lake. More often than not, Red Lake is utterly dry. It is a huge bed of salts evaporated out of floodwaters. Mud cracks lie 20 yards wide. Today there is water across some of the lake, a shallow film in driven sheets, a collection of recent flooding. We fly beyond Red Lake toward the Peacock Mountains, over the stretched grid-like pattern of the Burlington Northern Santa Fe railroad tracks. A freight train heads north beneath us. Railroad tracks are planted straight across the desert, damming a long line of flood courses. I make notes on this.

I tap the pilot's shoulder and point ahead. She flies east from the tracks. Down from the theater of the Peacock Mountains spreads a hundred small washes. I shout to her, asking if she will fly as low as she can along the washes. These are the washes that sometimes deliver floods toward the railroad tracks where the water is briefly imprisoned before it cuts its way through any weakness it can find. For 15 minutes we streak over these winding bands of drainages while I write in my notebook. Then we turn and land at the airport just outside of Kingman.

Dan Barkhurst, an officer with the Kingman Fire Department, meets me there. We shake hands, and I climb into his truck. We head north, toward a recent flash flood site where he had been involved as a rescuer. As we drive, he tells me stories from his childhood in this region.

"I remember being stuck in Lake Havasu City for hours because all of the roads were under water," he says, looking at me now and then

from behind the steering wheel. "We knew how to avoid floods. The problem now is that there are so many more people living here and they don't all know about floods. In almost every big storm, someone tries to drive across a wash. Nobody wants to wait for the floods to subside. They have no idea what kind of power they are dealing with."

He is taking me to a flood site, the scene of both a remarkable disaster and a rare miracle. We turn off the paved road, the old Route 66, onto not really a dirt road, just an opening out to the desert. Mud flings up and slaps against the sides of the truck. We stop just before the train tracks. I get out. Within a few steps, 3-inch platform soles of soaked clay are stuck to my boots.

The desert around here is remarkably bare, with only four types of plants in view anywhere — cholla cactus, banana yucca, saltbush, and tumbleweed — and not many of them. We walk to the track where a minor bridge has been completely rebuilt after a flood crippled it. On the other side of the bridge is a dilapidated barbed wire fence with a few pieces of police tape still fluttering like wings in the occasional breeze. Beyond that stands an elevated cattle tank. I climb up to the cattle tank to have a look around, but I can't get up high enough to see the spread of local washes. The ground looks flat and impervious to flooding. I need the airplane back. From here I see none of the order that was revealed from the air.

A freight train pounds through, filling the desert air with noise and friction. The tumbleweeds along the track bend against artificial wind. I reach down and snatch up some of the mud and clay, rubbing it between my fingers. The train is long, an amazing amount of weight moving at 90 miles per hour. I think, if this train were to hit a flood . . .

I stand waiting for the train to pass. Only half an hour ago, from the plane I had been able to clearly see the paths of floods. Now with this cattle tank and barbed wire, with the railroad bridge, with the train barreling by, with the smoothness of the desert, I can see why a person might never think a flood could touch this place. I even start to wonder myself. The bright police tape now snaps furiously in the wind.

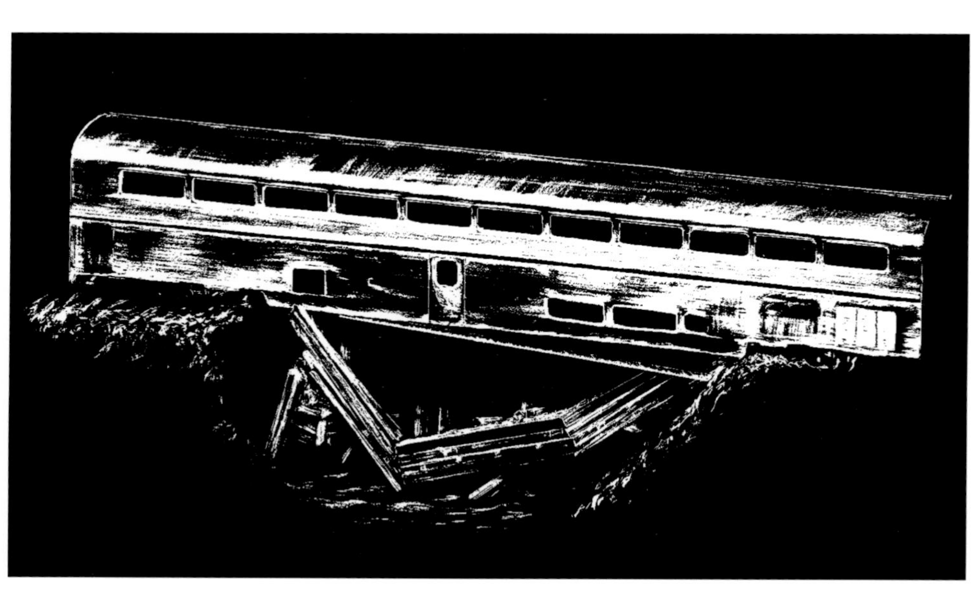

AUGUST 9

In Los Angeles, the train's manifest lists 294 passengers and 18 crew members. The train is the Southwest Chief, now turning around for its trip back to Chicago and running a little behind schedule.

The train is rich with history: The turquoise that once decorated the walls of one of its dining cars in the 1920s now resides in a prominent museum collection.

In the town of Gallup, New Mexico, two Navajo women are scheduled to board. Wearing turquoise jewelry and delicious velvet dresses, they are hired to give informative talks about the people of the region and are to be dropped off in Albuquerque as the train continues northeast.

The train has no accidents to its name.

There is no rain as people board, pulling their carry-on luggage up through the narrow doors. The summer air is oppressively hot outside, even with the sun low.

Inside the air-conditioned cars, the passengers inhale the wonderfully cooled air. By 7:15 in the evening, the train is just leaving the city as everyone settles in. The sleeping car attendants have already turned down the beds and are preparing to come around to answer questions, to smile and nod and make certain that everyone is comfortable. The conductor comes through collecting tickets. He goes door to door in the sleeping cars and along the chairs in coach, his hand reaching out ritualistically, waiting and open for the next ticket.

Passing Barstow a few hours later, the train rolls beneath an open sky of stars. Many passengers are asleep. Some are still in the lounge car, winding down their conversations with strangers, enjoying the details of other people's lives, people they will never see again. The train is now even further behind schedule, an hour already. Slower freight trains ahead have been the problem. Whenever the track is clear of them, the Southwest Chief's engineer throttles up to 90 miles per hour, regulation top speed.

North of the Old Woman Mountains in the desert of western California, the first rain comes as a wall. The train's skin shudders as if passing into a solid object. Inside the cars, a steely hiss rises over the sound of the tracks. Some people wake to the change. They feel around in the dark, sit up, and then realize that it is only rain. They go back to sleep.

This night, wind has been up around 80 miles per hour. A flash flood earlier hit the outskirts of the Arizona town of Kingman, where helicopters rescued two people off the roofs of their stranded vehicles.

This wall of rain has been on the move all night and into the morning. People who have been manning the satellite computers are ready to give way to the incoming day shift. These exhausted weather watchers

have been tracking thunderheads back and forth across the borders of Arizona, Nevada, and California throughout the night, then making calls and typing out messages before returning to check the monitor screens again. They have been sending out flash flood warnings much of the night, leap-frogging their messages across counties.

Rain, when it comes to this desert, falls out of the sky like bricks. Storms hit the ground and are gone. Even satellites can lose the trail as thunderheads bloom out of nothing and disappear.

In the coming morning, a truck will be found cocked on its side — the driver's door hanging open and draped with flood debris — in a drying wash near Kingman. A flood pushed the abandoned truck off of a nearby road that crosses the wash. The driver, a 41-year-old woman, will be found the next day a few miles downstream, her lifeless body half-buried in sand and mud.

All night, storms had jumped from Kingman to Las Vegas, Nevada, and back. They filled Las Vegas streets with water, washed cars away, and toppled power lines. Then, wiping their hands clean of violence, the storms lifted and vanished. Their faint blue flashes of lightning trailed into the distance. But the storms never went far before touching ground again. Shortly after the Las Vegas floods, storms erupted to the south at Lake Havasu City, Arizona, and again the cars turned into boats. Rescuers worked into the night pulling people out. Then fresh thunderheads built once more over Las Vegas, sending water back down the drying streets.

The night went on like this, thunderheads building, dumping, and fading in an hour's time, or even in 15 minutes. Each time a storm would leave, silence settled in, a pure, unadulterated quiet that made the previous storm seem impossible. Abandoned cars rested sideways along streets that now carried only trickles of leftover rainwater. With the power out in parts of Las Vegas, stars reflected brilliantly against wet asphalt.

At 3 A.M., the Southwest Chief stops in the desert town of Needles, California.

Electricity still serves the town because crews have been out repairing a transformer struck by lightning. The sky is strangely clear in Needles. There is no sign of rain, except when the train doors open and the strong smell of a desert thunderstorm enters the cars. It is a newborn scent, sweet with creosote bushes and the steaminess of cold water against hot earth.

Needles still shimmers from a recent rain, a gully washer the locals call it. The man working the station complains to the Southwest Chief's conductor, saying it's been raining off and on like all hell's broken loose. And now nothing. The last storm headed northeast. He points that way, as if relieved to be free of it.

The train starts up again. First there is a forward jolt that brings most people awake for just a second. Then a couple of lesser surges, and the train is moving freely, heading northeast.

An hour or so before the Southwest Chief reaches western Arizona's Hualapai Valley, the Burlington Northern Santa Fe tracks are deluged in rain. This particular thunderhead gathers around the nearby Peacock Mountains as if taking up residence, hurling pulsing rain down at the desert.

A light appears on the tracks below the mountains. The beam, slivered by rain, is accompanied by the sliding rattle of steel wheels. A spotlight sweeps the ground, dipping to one side, then the other.

The light and sound come from a railroad vehicle sent ahead to check the tracks because flood warnings had dictated that the line be surveyed in person. The vehicle, a truck hoisted onto drop-down track wheels, slows as it crosses each trestle. A track inspector shines the light into the bare washes below. Everything looks good. No sign of flooding or damage. The vehicle keeps on, its red tail lights becoming smaller, more faint, and the noise of its wheels fading into the pulse of the storm.

The thunderhead rises with hot updrafts off the back of the Peacock Mountains, scattering lightning inside of its own folds. The rain up there comes too fast to soak back into any of the small springs. It is like dumping a bucket. The water grows.

Small floods seek every possible wash, crack, arroyo, rill, and hole off the flanks of the Peacocks. They flow around tight bundles of drought grass until the grass uproots. Objects such as bones or branches either impede the water flow or gather into the momentum and are carried

away. Any grass available to hold the water back is bunched and isolated. Rainwater runs across bare rock and cascades into larger and larger accumulations.

Thus orchestrated, larger floods emerge from the Peacock Mountains, running through a washboard of drainages. By the time they pour to a lower elevation, they have settled into a matrix of atavistic flood channels. These courses form a web over the entire desert slope beneath the mountains, sorting water with ancient familiarity.

The front edges of these floods snap and growl with debris — pieces of manzanita, fallen juniper branches, coarse gravel. They are foamy, gurgling shelves that slow down, stagnate, and abruptly quicken. They gather into a broad wave that sweeps the desert, caroming into the Burlington Northern Santa Fe tracks, which lie at a 90-degree angle to the water.

The flood courses northeast along the tracks until it can fall into an arroyo and pass under its only exit, a channel under a small bridge called 504.1S in railroad lingo. The entire surrounding desert feeds its water into this narrow passage, a funnel too small for the volumn. The channel gulps and gasps, trying to swallow the flood and pass it through. Fast, rumbling water surrounds the bridge's support timbers. Rising 8 feet to the underside of the tracks, the water shakes the timbers. Critical parts of this 75-year-old wooden bridge weaken. Bank walls cave in, sucked under in dark roils. Buried timber foundations are swept open and carried away. It is 4:45 A.M.

At just about 5 o'clock, the Southwest Chief settles into top speed after the latest stop in Kingman, Arizona. There was no time wasted, but the train is now an hour and a half behind schedule. The dining compartment, decorated with fresh flowers and linen, is closed until breakfast. The car attendants are just getting about their early tasks, arranging newspapers that they will slip under the cabin doors. Passengers who are awake on the Southwest Chief this morning roll through the desert, looking out into predawn darkness as the rain tapers off. They can see lightning outlining the Peacock Mountains in the distance.

Just 150 feet from the bridge, the engineer glimpses a sag in the line. The tracks are warping downward, and they begin to buckle before his eyes. Below the misshapen tracks, he sees a flood, and he hits the emergency brake. The train is too close. Crossing the damaged bridge at 90 miles per hour, three locomotives uncouple. They break free from the remainder of the train, actually leaving the tracks only to fall back into place.

As the following cars pass, flood-weakened timbers collapse. The bridge explodes beneath the weight, hurling wood into the flood. Sixteen cars jump the track as the bulk of the Southwest Chief goes from 90 miles per hour to a complete stop in six seconds.

Train accidents are nothing like car accidents. There is so much momentum that steel disintegrates on impact, weight from behind still racing forward at full speed. Sturdy lengths of iron track twist as if made of hot plastic. Blocks of solid oak railroad ties rupture into splinters, chewed into the machinery. In a blizzard of sparks, a half-ton axle sails

away to plant into the wet earth like a javelin. People in their beds fly into the ceilings like rag dolls without even a moment to wake. In coach class, people are ripped from their seats, thrown row after row toward the front.

The two passenger cars ahead of the bridge jackknife into each other, hinging 20 feet off the track. Two locomotives plow to one side, leaving the third to roll ahead, uncoupled and alone. Portions of track peel back and vivisect the baggage car. Arriving cars slam into one another in rhythm.

At last, the train does not move, compressed and cantilevered as it is amid the jumble of rails and ties. Now there is no rumble of wheels on tracks, only the sounds of injured people shouting, of panicked passengers struggling toward exits in the dark, and of the surging hiss of flood waters. Lights are out in most of the cars. Some people find flashlights. They kick at the metal doors and windows to open them. In one car, a group finds an emergency sledgehammer and breaks down the door, only to find their car suspended 12 feet above the ground. Part of the bridge hangs 45 degrees into the flood, forming a steep rapids, while a sleeping car spans the arroyo where the bridge had been. In the first faint light, passengers emerge from the sleeping car with desperate hesitancy, balancing over the flood on what remains of the opposite, westbound track. They grab the side of the train for support, taking one step at a time to get out, and fix their eyes on the dark water and foam rushing beneath their feet.

Amid the wreckage, 116 people are injured. People from all over the continent, but most have never been to a desert. Those still able to walk get out into the morning heat, into the smell of wetness. Tossed into an ironic, vacuous land, they mill aimlessly about the wreckage. This train is famous for the scenery it passes through, being promoted like a traveling postcard. These people walk around in the irony, face to face with the desert. Sirens sound from the distance.

Without pause, the water passes from below the Peacock Mountains and looks for still farther channels. The water is beyond tearing away the last of the bridge and the sleeping car above it. As it is now, the water will travel to the sand dunes, fanning window glass and sheared steel bolts into the desert. Out there, as the flood spreads into the sand, the desert steals the precise definitions of water courses. There will be no destination for this water. It will not reach the Colorado River by this path. It will not sustain cattle or be pumped into bottles to be sold as drinking water. No corn or cottonseed or soy will grow from it. There will be no legal battles between states as to who owns it. The water ebbs and vanishes — evaporates or sinks — before the last passenger is taken from the Southwest Chief in a stretcher. No one has died. Some say that it is a miracle.

The decision-makers come a few hours after the rescuers. They stand in the damp wash and look up at the damage. An FBI official is flown in. He walks up to the fire chief from Kingman and asks his opinion on what happened.

The fire chief, Chuck Osterman, who has been awake since midnight on flood rescues, regards the FBI man. Osterman is exhausted and not in the mood for someone seeking complicated answers to a simple question.

"Looks like it rained hard, flooded, and the bridge failed. Then the train came," he tells the federal agent.

The FBI man nods stoically, thinking that he will have to find his answers elsewhere.

For those officials and engineers brought from other states, other climates, the desert must seem peculiar. The flood must seem a lie. Pieces of track and splintered timbers are now scattered across the desert plain miles beyond, unaccountably abandoned in curious, desolate places that are already almost dry.

HAVASU CANYON, GRAND CANYON

Walking to my knees in clear water, I pull a wooden dory against a slight current, rope dragging over my bare shoulder. Clean sand parts beneath my feet. The dory's oars are stowed. The canyon is barely wide enough to fit through. Sunlight hits the water and sends a web of reflected light against the curving rock walls. The web undulates, mirroring gentle eddies and curls in the stream below. A woman standing in the dory extends her hands, pushing off to make sure the wood of the boat does not scrape against the hard, pale sandstone.

The walls around me are polished smooth by floods, turned and torqued by the water. The dory wants to slide into a hollow in the rock. The woman's right hand gently touches stone, directing the boat away. This is where water does its work. Even in today's calm flow, the passage of a flood is distinctively evident. Floods run wild in here. Their mark is not violent nor grotesque. The mark is beautifully done, rock carved with orderliness, as clean and alluring as the inside of a shell.

The Grand Canyon is arranged like the roots of a tree. The Colorado

River is the meandering main stock and from it hundreds of lesser canyons branch outward. These canyon roots wind for 10 or 20 or 50 miles, branching into more and more feeder canyons, some dry and others graced with creeks like this one. Each of these roots, almost every year, will carry a flash flood, sending it down to the river. A man who rows dories in the Grand Canyon once told me about trying to outrun a flood in one of these canyons. He had left his dory tied at the mouth of a side canyon that flashed while he was hiking. He raced down and launched himself into the boat. Before he could get it untied, the water

came. His dory jerked against moored lines, hit with tree parts, red mud slopping over the gunwales. He couldn't untie the lines, of course. They were so taut they were singing. He touched the ropes with a knife blade, and they snapped into the air. His dory reeled out of the side canyon floodwaters into the river.

With the rope in my hand, I look for a place to tie off our dory. This is Havasu Creek, flowing down to the Colorado River in the center of the Grand Canyon. The confluence is a common stop along the river where rafts, kayaks, and dories turn out of the Colorado's fast, cold water into this clear-streamed side canyon, narrow as a city alley. There are bolts drilled into the walls where we tie off five dories and two rafts so the current won't push them back into the river. The space forms a tight parking lot, and we nose each boat into place, securing ropes to the bolts. Later in the day, around noon, this place will be packed with boats and people as numerous raft outfits come piling in, huge, 30-foot pontoon rafts tied off wherever there is purchase. This place ranks as a tourist attraction, the canyon of the blue water.

Far upstream from here is the village of Supai, the center of the Havasupai culture. The only way to reach it is on foot, by helicopter, or banging along on the back of a mule. Between here and there is a run of waterfalls and cascading streams.

We leave the dories and rafts, and, with day packs filled with lunch and simple supplies, we walk upstream. The water is peculiar. It is colored topaz, a strange hue that verges between cloudy and crisply clear. Most of the water comes from springs in the massive limestone formations of the Grand Canyon. Immaculate swimming water.

A few miles up, we unload our packs near a waterfall. The pool beyond it is the color of a robin's egg, clear into its depths. I dive in and swim across. The water is cool, not cold. My body is flustered by waves of air bubbles pulsing up from the waterfall. Turbulence increases nearer to the waterfall. It hurls round swells against the surface. I swim as hard as I can into the force, mist veiling my face when I lift my head to breathe.

I come around the side of the waterfall and snatch the bedrock wall with my hands. I hold on. My legs swing in the water, whipping like flags. Currents twist and snake across my body, winding up and down my spine, across my stomach. The waterfall, loud as a train, sends silver streaks of water into the air. Using the rock as a ladder I drag myself into the falls. It pounds on my head. No rhythm. Just sheets of hard, fast water. I keep pulling myself, my head sinking below the surface for a moment, ears socked in with air bubbles and the grumble of the waterfall.

When I lift my head, I am clear of the falls. I can breathe. I am behind the waterfall in an emerald room. The sunlight is subdued but mildly magnified, as if filtered through a stained glass window. The waterfall seals the room off completely.

The sound has no definition. A roar. I am inside of a pounding engine of water. I kick slowly, waving my arms to keep afloat. In front of me the waterfall against the sun looks like a wall of polished quartz. Veins of oxygen rake through too fast to watch.

The pool back here is slack, turning in a circle as slowly as the second hand on a clock. A raft of sticks has gathered in the far corner. One or two sticks venture toward me, then drift into the back again. They are slick and soaked. I gently paddle my way back through them, through a carpet of clean bubbles.

There is a remarkable equity to water. It gives and takes in equitable measures. This waterfall is here because a flood carved the earth just so. This water back here, perhaps it has not been replaced for months, the same water rotating easily like a globe, waiting for the next flood to come and send it out, flashing it down to where we left our dories. If a flood comes, what would it sound like in here? Could I somehow be safe in this merciful room?

As I float, I remember a flood in a canyon that like this seemed too luscious to be violent. I was there with a woman who was studying for her masters degree in desert water ecology. She wanted to show me a

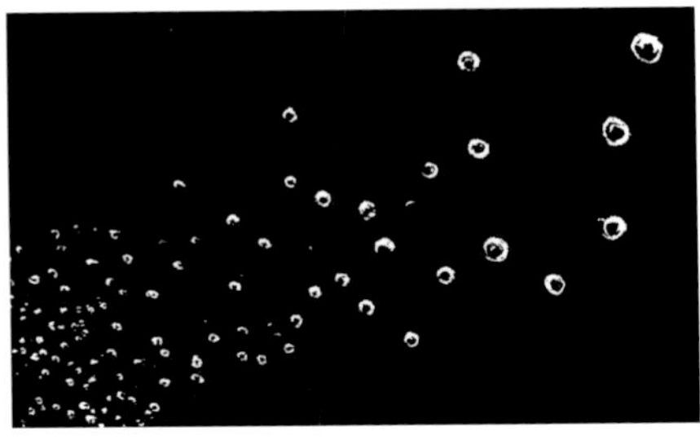

place she had found while doing research. Clean, running water shot down the canyon's center, and we swam against the current like spawning fish. There the canyon opened into smooth eggshell vaults of granite. I remember that she lay on the warm, sculpted rock, closing her eyes. I chased crawdads with a stick.

The storm hit us in the afternoon, breaking its back across the country above us. Her eyes fluttered open and she sat up. It was a July storm, the rain nearly horizontal, lightning cracking at the ground. Neither of us had taken note of the expanding clouds. We had even ignored the wind. Now we rushed to get out of there. At first, our movements were accompanied by laughter, a giddiness that comes with the first rain of the summer. We swam down the sleek, tubular passages. But the laughter then began to sound strained. The water rose around us as we swam and leapt into plunge pools. The stream picked up speed, turning dark, shoving at us. Pinches in the canyon floor blew us out like darts. When we reached a possible exit, we scrambled out of the coming flood, taking shelter beneath a low overhang. We wiped water out of our faces and watched. We were unhurt, not even scraped, but if we had remained any longer, the outcome would have been different.

The floods that come down Havasu Canyon are larger than most, far more powerful than the little flood that tumbled me and my friend from the granite canyon. Havasu drains more than 3,000 square miles of the Coconino Plateau around the southern portion of the Grand Canyon. The village of Supai has been flattened numerous times in floods, its buildings buckling and flushed down waterfalls.

The waterfalls themselves have been constantly reshaped by flooding. I once pored over a file of Havasu Canyon photographs taken in both the 1800s and the late 1900s. These were repeat photographs taken from exactly the same locations nearly a hundred years apart. Even over periods as short as three years, parts of the canyon did not look at all similar. Dry boulders were piled into places where there had previously been gentle cascades and clusters of cottonwood and ash trees. Entire

waterfalls came and went. I had never before seen the metamorphosis of a canyon so clearly. No monument could be saved. In a single flood, Havasu Falls itself carved nearly 30 feet deeper into the rimrock at the top.

The best example of change in Havasu Canyon is a place called Fiftyfoot Falls. The falls, downstream from Supai, have for the last 110 years been the most topographically unstable in the canyon, responding markedly to erosion and to being plugged by flash flood debris. While some historical accounts have suggested that a single 1932 flash flood from an unnamed tributary created the entire falls, photographs of the region dating back to 1885 show that Fiftyfoot Falls has been gouged into existence and then smoothed over numerous times. Photographer Josef Muench reported the falls as a prominent feature in 1937, then found them to have been completely destroyed by floods by 1939. They are back in existence today.

This room behind the waterfall is transient, like any of the rooms, boulders, and waterfalls of Havasu. It might only be a couple of years old. I slip through the jade light at the back of the chamber, sticks and air bubbles jostling lightly around my shoulders. I push myself out through the waterfall. The impact shoves me underwater, tumbling my body. I am shot into the clear of the pool, my body surfacing and drifting away like a boat cut loose. I climb onto the smooth, dry trunk of a fallen cottonwood tree. There I spread out, letting my hands dangle into the slow current. The thorny underbark of the tree pokes into my stomach and my thighs. The sun is bright on my skin. Beads of water slide across my back, pearls falling into the water.

Of the 14 major floods to strike Havasu in the past hundred years, 12 occurred during summer thunderstorms. But that is not reason enough to relax during the winter. Of those 15 floods, the three largest came during the winter. Summer storms are sudden and violent, the floods short-lived. They derive from convective thunderstorms, bales of heat shooting off the ground, colliding with cold upper-atmospheric air to create islands of cumulus nimbus clouds. In the winter, the storms are huge, slow, frontal systems, their rains long-lasting. Winter floods build over time, greatly exceeding the volume of summer floods.

Beginning at the very end of the 1800s, peaking with a massive winter flood in 1910, Havasu Canyon was physically rearranged by water in dramatic ways until the 1940s. Then came a curious hiatus in heavy flooding from 1940 to 1990, allowing vegetation to establish itself and numerous, spectacular travertine deposits to form. The famous, otherworldly pools of Havasu Falls with rimstone dams and orderly cascades were formed in this time.

On September 3, 1990, the pause ended. A typical, late-summer low pressure system in California collided over Arizona with moist Pacific air from the eastern Mexican coast and dumped into Havasu Creek. Suddenly, a 14-foot wall of water came down on the village of Supai. The flood went on, gathering thousands of trees from the canyon floor,

launching them into the Colorado River. The luxurious travertine dams around the base of Havasu Falls, photographed for postcards and travel brochures, were mostly obliterated.

This was the beginning of a new flood series that has yet to end. Like trying on new clothes, Havasu Canyon changed shape from flood to flood after this 1990 restart. Predicting these floods has not been easy or successful. Eleven of the 14 major floods in the last century occurred in association with an El Niño cycle, but the mid-century gap in large floods is hard to explain. Long-term global weather patterns are as influential as day-long local weather systems, neither of which are especially well understood.

In the afternoon, I leave the waterfall and walk back toward the Colorado River. Eventually I meet up with the others from the dories. In the last mile, I give them my pack to carry so that I can swim the final distance to the river. I enter the creek, which alternates between quiet, reflective pools and swift runs turning into short waterfalls. I sweep into these like an abandoned leaf, my shoulder blades breaching the fast, smooth water at the crest of a falls. Turned heels over head, I drop and emerge in a pool below. Within half an hour of this tumble play, I reach the narrowest part of the canyon. The shadow of my body slips across the pale blue floor far beneath me. I ripple over the stones and slide like a ghost across sand. The canyon closes around me.

There are voices ahead. I can't see the people yet, but I hear the chatter, the clanking of metal. Ice chests opening and closing. The squeak of skin on the wet rubber of a raft. When I drift into view, the canyon is a zoo of humanity. Kayaks are stuffed into spaces between behemoth rafts. People toss objects back and forth, stepping from one boat to the next, stowing life vests, gathering gear for hikes. One guide sits back on a raft tube, a magazine opened over her face. She turns the page.

I am only a disembodied head floating through. The rest of me is underwater. I tend toward the slim space between two rafts, under the guide with the magazine. I try to see what she's reading, but too quickly

I am past her. A loaf of sliced bread is out on the next raft, mustard being spread, sandwiches passed out. Laughter fills the sandstone room. A joke somewhere. Our original small fleet of dories is penned in by more and more boats. There must be three different commercial outfits here and a few private boaters, too. Most of the people are gone, maybe a hundred tourists heading in surges up Havasu Canyon for a hike. The people remaining are mostly guides or people who've been on the oars all day, too tired to go walking.

The water goes shallow across the sand, and I let my body spread flat with my heels poking out behind me. I reach the opening where Havasu Creek meets the Colorado River. The river swirls toward me, crossing me with its muddy ice water. I grab a line hanging off one of the rafts and stop, bobbing against the tension of the rope. I can see out to the river. Thirty-foot J-rig rafts with outboard motors are parallel parked, tied one after the next to the dark, cliffy shoreline.

This small creek's sensitivity is replaced by the river's headlong roll. The Colorado River moves forward as if on important business, fast, dark, and cold. Its voice is grumbling and professorial compared to the lustrous pitch of the creek. The confluence, the meeting of waters, is an enchanting place. One class of water here comes from as far away as the Wind River Range in Wyoming and from the Front Range of the Rockies in Colorado, the other from a local high desert plateau. They are two different species of water joining. If the river itself was to flood, it would rise slowly from mountain snowmelt. Rapids would change their shape, some smeared over, others made more difficult. On the other hand, if Havasu Canyon floods, there will be a compressed maelstrom bursting into this corridor like an angry giant unleashed, pounding from wall to wall.

At this point of contact, boats gather like bees on a hive. People's voices bounce off the close walls. I cling to a rope between the two places, feeling ribbons of contrary water looping around my body.

AUGUST 10

Some of those who live in this canyon bear last names old enough to have been given to geologic formations in the Grand Canyon. There are the family names of Watahomigi and Wescogame, both of which are also names for rock layers within the Supai formation. In the Havasupai langauge, the tribe's name, Ha vasúa báaja, *is a direct reference to the mineral blue color of the water. The people here have tied themselves so closely to the landscape that they are literally imbedded within it, their village tucked into one of the deeper canyons of the Grand Canyon. They know well enough the ability of the desert to flood. Stock animals have perished in the canyon's droughts, countered with the 20 horses killed in the 1910 flood that erased the village, even the stone schoolhouse. Traditionally, a year's worth of food was stored on the rim by this Havasupai culture. Not just seed corn for the next phase of crops, but actual edible goods. Storing food was done out of obligation, a way of bowing the head in understanding. To live below the walls of Havasu Canyon and believe you were immune from catastrophe would be an arrogance beyond comprehension.*

Of any day, today is when Havasu Canyon is most populated: the very end of the annual Peach Festival. Some 200 tourists have hiked and helicoptered in to join the regular population of 600 local Havasupai residents. The canyon's minutiae — the cottonwood trees, fat boulders, and waterfalls — seem most permanent with everyone here watching. No one thinks of a flood.

Mike Moore pilots a tour helicopter on a scheduled flight with three passengers from the South Rim's Grand Canyon Heliport to Supai. As he swings over the canyon rim near Supai, he hesitates, seeing a thunderstorm pouring into his destination. The inside of the canyon is violet-dark. He lands on the plateau above instead. Lightning shatters the edges of the storm. They wait. It looks like a boiling soup down there, wind ripping apart the outside of the storm, hurling torn pieces of cloud up onto the rim.

Moore jokes that they might be the first to see the flood of '97. After half an hour, there is a space in the storm. He flies into the hole to land at Supai.

Most of the village is under muddy, swift water. Passing over, he sees that some of the buildings are gone. The campground is missing entirely. The plumbing and sewage system has been ripped out of the ground like an exhumed skeleton. Farther from the center of the village, toward the middle of the canyon, the bulk of the flood pushes through, striking over even the largest trees. He lands at a dry, protected place and unloads the three passengers.

Quickly, he is besieged. Another tour helicopter has already been employed, lifting people out of the tops of trees that have not yet fallen.

A Havasupai woman in a dress waits in high branches for the helicopter to come, her tree shivering against the flood.

A man who works unloading baggage and one of the Council elders jump into Moore's helicopter. They point the way for him to go. The elder, a man named Lester Crooke, wears mud up his clothes nearly to his neck. He tells Moore that they heard the flood coming, getting enough warning that people in Supai had time to get to safety. But he is worried about people downstream who will not have so much warning.

First they fly around the rim to see how much more water is coming down. Waterfalls lace the cliffs. The flood is not slowing. They drop back into the canyon, passing over people stranded near the campground. Two people cling to a cottonwood's upper branches, only 8 feet above the floodwaters. The other helicopter busily gathers survivors with a rope, hauling them off to high ground.

Moore and his crew pass the village, heading downstream to follow the flood. He makes a last call into the heliport. He lets the dispatcher know he is running low on fuel and that he is on his way down to warn hikers if he can. Then the radio cuts out. From between the cliff walls of the inner canyon, only static will come back through the radio.

The helicopter shoots past waterfalls. Parts of buildings sweep over each other below them. A picnic table plunges 190 feet over Mooney Falls. In only a few minutes, Moore overtakes the front edge of the flood. Downstream, the calm water is colored turquoise. The flood gobbles up the color, filling it with fast, fuming mud. It is not really a wave at the front. It is more like huge knuckles of water and debris working into each other. They are full of trees and lumber from houses taken out upstream. The flood cuts the corner of every bend, slapping over boulders and sloshing against the outside cliff walls. Moore figures that the leading edge is moving at about 40 miles per hour. He dips the helicopter closer, racing ahead of the flood.

The nearer Moore comes to the Colorado River, the narrower the canyon becomes. Now 36 years old, he has been flying since he was 16. For two summers he ran a helicopter in Alaska, landing in places barely larger than the helicopter itself. Although this Havasu flight is breathtakingly tight for Crooke and the baggage man, Moore feels that he still has plenty of room to operate. The helicopter peels around corners, tipping on edge.

Down the canyon, it is a hot, beautiful day. The sun is out in a clear sky. A good day for swimming. There is no sign of a coming flood. Three minutes out from under the storm, Moore comes upon the first hikers from the Colorado River. They don't know about the flood or even the storm upstream. Moore drops as close to the canyon floor as he can safely get. The baggage man in the back opens the door and leans out.

The hikers are angry, offended, waving them away. This is the typical relationship between hikers and tour helicopters. Their hike is ruined by the scream of rotors. But quickly they take an interest in the hand signals given to them. The baggage man points upstream, stabbing the air with his hand. They look upstream. It must seem absurd to them, but

the message is clear: GET OUT OF HERE. *They wave back briskly and scramble for high ground.*

Each batch of hikers reacts the same way. Anger, then curiosity, then realization. A few of the hikers are caught swimming naked in transparent pools. Some have high open ground for an escape. Others are trapped in narrow, bedrock pens with cliffs all around them. All Moore can do is hang his helicopter over their heads, while Crooke and the baggage man lean out the doors and wave their arms. The people in the narrows have few choices. They begin clawing at the rock walls, falling, and helping each other up ledge by ledge. Some crawl onto a high boulder in the middle of the canyon, hoping they can ride its peak through the flood.

Downstream, Havasu Canyon merges with the Colorado River. Blue water flows through a strikingly narrow stretch of canyon before emptying into the Colorado. River guides call the place Have-a-Zoo *rather than Havasu. This time of the day in the summer it is a spectacle of tied-off rafts stuffed as far into the side canyon as they can get, out of the flow of the Colorado River. Two companies, Wilderness River Adventures and Western Rivers, have their six boats nosed straight into the flow of Havasu Creek. A private group is in too. A canoe and nine kayaks have been shimmied along the 6-foot-wide slot, parked near the first waterfall.*

Bret Stark, a guide for Wilderness, cradles the back of his head in his hands, legs propped over the oars, his eyes closed. Upstream, 28 of his clients are hiking in the narrow enclosures with most of the guides. Contour lines of refracted light paint the walls.

As helicopters do over canyons, this one comes out of nowhere. Stark jumps. He sees Crooke, the tribal chairman, leaning from the passenger door of the helicopter. He sees that the man's clothes are matted with mud. Crooke gives frantic hand signals, pointing fiercely upstream. The remaining guides down below scramble, shouting and climbing, to get the hell off the boats. They throw ropes and grab what gear they can, personal belongings snatched off the decks. Once everyone is clear, there is a waiting silence. The water coming out of the canyon is blue as ever. The boats hover serenely above their shadows. There is no telling how close the flood is.

Moore takes his helicopter out to the Colorado River and hovers about 15 feet off the water. He faces directly toward the entrance of Havasu. The view is like a movie screen. He watches the guides throwing ropes and gear, climbing the walls to get out. He waits.

In the deceiving upcanyon quiet, some of the guides decide to climb back down and get a few of the rafts untied, cautiously moving them away from Havasu. The first raft is taken out. A man pulls on the oars toward the river. He checks over his shoulder to navigate the boat, but keeps snapping his head back toward the upstream canyon, thinking he hears a roar. He does not want to be caught in his raft. Then he reaches the river. He is free of the creek and its thin canyon, free of the impending flood. He is out, relieved to be taken by the river's current.

One of the guides returning to the boats is Okie, one of the commercial head guides. Even under clear skies, with some clouds to the north, he had arrived with apprehension today. On his order, the usual half-day hike had been cut to an hour. He had sensed a flood — why, he cannot say — and did not want to take the risk by sending people on a hike deep into the canyon. But his customers are up there right now. He hopes they know what the helicopter meant. There is nothing he can do to help them now. He works with several others, getting another raft pulled out and to the river, away from the coming flood.

The quiet is unnerving. Something is about to explode. They work without speaking, untangling lines and prying out knots from another raft. Okie looks up suddenly. Midway through a knot, Stark looks up too. Voices come down the canyon. Screams. Everyone on the boats stands absolutely still, listening. The voices come closer, like birds warning each other through a forest. Only these sound utterly terrified. No one is untying anything. No one is moving. Then the voices are swallowed by a roar.

One of the guides, standing on a boat farthest into the canyon, swings around. "IT'S HERE! NOW! GET OUT!"

Okie jumps and lands on the nose of a 22-foot snout raft. He grabs an extra life vest and turns upstream, frozen for just another second. The topaz water of Havasu Creek jerks upward. Water beneath it is red and abruptly tall. For half a second the two waters are separate, like a double-layered cake. Then the red breaks in, pushing out the blue. He cuts his stare and leaps from one raft to the next, across six neatly lined rafts. Springing off the last, he lands on a ledge. The boats rupture behind him.

Pat Phillips, another guide, is just the same, caught for that second. He cannot help it, gripped by this sudden apparition. In his only free moment, he stares down the throat of a canyon flood, a liquid wall full of trees coming around the corner. The sight is so overwhelmingly momentous that only one detail stands out — the smell. Compost and violence and crushed rocks. A stray thought flits by. Death, he thinks. It smells like death. *He jumps out before the flood hits him.*

Knots reach their breaking point in the water. Lines snap without hesitation. Boats flip, piling against each other — two fully loaded 22-foot snout boats, three 18-foot Canyon rafts, several other large boats. Deck canoes, kayaks, and uprooted trees blow out like confetti. Mooring ropes break. Rocks break. Not one object holds against the water. A 30-foot-long tree trunk slams into one of the rafts.

This sudden flume of water holds no delicacies or innuendoes. Guides perch on ledges, emergency throw lines clutched tight in their hands. They wait for bodies, bodies of people they know, the clients and other guides who were hiking upstream. Debris flushes into the river, a river that is large enough so that the flood hardly alters its volume. Ice chests and spare oars sweep out of the canyon.

Stark, with his life vest cinched so tight his rib cage barely expands to his breath, doubts that many have survived. The bodies, *he thinks.*

How will we deal with so many bodies? *He stands with feet apart, preparing to throw his line in case anyone should appear alive.*

Clothes come down in the froth, pieces of equipment. Each time they see color, they panic. Calves tighten to jump. "No, no!" *somebody shouts.* "It's just a shirt!"

They wait.

An Arizona Department of Public Safety helicopter arrives. Circling the next rafting outfit downstream on the Colorado River, the message from its bullhorn is simple.

HAVASU FLASHED. BE READY FOR BOATS AND BODIES.

In a froth of whirling debris just beyond the confluence, boats are stacked and cocked sideways, drifting downstream. No bodies show. The guides on the cliffs keep waiting, but their muscles relax after a while. On the throw lines, their hands loosen.

The flood retains its peak for almost four hours. After six hours, they are able to set ropes from one side to the next, slowly recovering people trapped on boulders and ledges. The people who had taken to the big midstream boulder are still crouched, clinging, as if their perch might still sink, their eyes wild with fear.

A head count is taken before dark. Between private and commercial river groups, the number is 80. No one is missing. In fact, there is one person too many. Another count is made, and still it is one person over. Outfitters can laugh at this now, at the idea of someone sneaking up on with them. There will be no bodies. No one has died.

Lost boats are retrieved and motored back upstream by other outfits. Park Service rescuers unload emergency military rations by helicopter and pass on the word that, somehow, no one was killed at the village.

Every element had been primed for the largest flood disaster in Grand Canyon's history. Getting a helicopter down the canyon, breaking flight zone regulations and radio rules, was doubtless the one act that changed the course of events. It is widely agreed that without Mike Moore's remarkable flight, many would have died. The guides waiting downstream would have been caught unawares as trees and a wall of water came down on them at 40 miles per hour. Crooke's and the baggage man's hand gestures sent each last hiker climbing the walls. A 50-year-old junior high band director from Ohio, with a proven fear of heights, had spidered 60 feet up the wall, taking handholds that shocked even the guides.

Getting him down would be a 90-minute-long technical rescue.

The next day, a Park Service raft lands at Havasu Canyon from the Colorado River. Several rangers disembark to clean the remains of raft debris. One man reaches for a snapped polypropylene rope leading to a metal bolt in the rock. A life vest had been clipped into the same bolt. He tries to work out the knot with his fingers to separate the two, but he can't. He comes close to get a better look. The life vest and rope had ridden out the entire flood, swirling against each other for hours.

When he gets the knot in his hands, he is startled to find that heat from underwater friction had actually melted the rope and vest together. He pulls a knife and cuts away the melted mass.

ANTELOPE CANYON

Few people ever witness a big flood in the desert. Most watch them blaze down the streets of Phoenix or Las Vegas. They watch them carve away sidewalks, thumping cars broadside along highways, loading driveways full of gravel. People see downed eucalyptus trees and local businesses with their carpets ruined by water. The damage is repaired as quickly as insurance claims adjusters and backhoe crews arrive. Fresh paint and masonry mask any sign of flooding.

In the wilderness, the backhoes do not come. There are no repairs. The relationship between water and earth is made more clear. It is an evolution instead of a natural disaster.

Since you may not have the opportunity to see a flood in action, the next best thing is to see what the flood leaves behind. Go into a canyon and have a look around. Touch things. Pick up rocks and feel how they've been worn. Study the rippled, dune-like patterns of sand, gravel, and dry mud on the floor. Run your hands along the walls to feel where turbulence reached its peak in the hollowed-out cavity of an alcove. Especially in the narrow canyons that stand like fossilized floods, this is where water truly gets about its business, revealing intimate details about the life of water. Walking in these places is like tracking an animal, studying the finesse of its prints. One place that I recommend for this view of a flood is a slot canyon named Antelope Canyon. It is a thin fissure in the bedrock of far northern Arizona, a tourist attraction on the Navajo Reservation.

I am standing over this crevice of Antelope, looking inside. It is dark down there, as if I am looking through the cracked roof of a mosque into an unlit interior. A metal ladder leads down and I follow it. There are others with me, friends. We paid $17.50 each to a reservation concessionaire to enter. We wait, one at a time. There is hardly enough room to squeeze inside. On the rim above, a hand-painted sign warns of flash flood danger.

Below the surface of the wash, inside of the crack, the ground spreads open. The ladders lead down farther, the canyon turning to a cavern. It is indeed a cave. It as a canyon underground. The sun is mostly shut out, the air suddenly cold. There is only one reason such a deep, slender canyon is here. Floods have carved it, leaving a thin space down within the bedrock. Its walls are sheer and close together, like the walls

of two tall buildings almost touching, leaving barely enough room to walk through. Draped through the grates and bars of the metal steps are streamers of flood debris. Small stones are jammed into the spaces, forced down by pressure. The power of water on earth has never been so clear or so graceful. But for now, it is completely dry.

Sweeping in and out of each other, the rock walls look more like fabric than stone. The canyon slides around itself, a hall of mirrors. Huge fins and condyles of sandstone hang overhead, hundreds of tons of rock supported by nothing but curves. I walk. Slowly. The next ladder appears, and I drop farther, pausing so that I don't step on the head of the person below me.

In the desert, the two primary elements are stone and water. Stone comes in abundance, exposed by weathering and a lack of vegetation. It is a canvas. Water crosses this stone with such rarity and ferocity that it tells all of its secrets in the shapes left behind. Antelope Canyon's interior is the pure expression of both.

None of us have been in here before. We use trite adjectives when we talk. "Astounding," "beautiful," "unbelievable." They are the only words we can find. It is a caricature of a canyon, each feature swollen to grandiose proportions. Our bodies appear and disappear around the bends. My head tilts back as the canyon deepens by a couple hundred feet. I am wondering if a human artist could ever reproduce something like this. In what media? Perhaps marble polished by hand, or maybe silk. Down in the midday darkness, far too dim to even read, I see a tiny patch of something that almost resembles light on the wall above me. It is maybe a slight variation in the color of rock. I reach up and touch it. It is sunlight reflected and reshaped before getting this far down, turned into a slight stain on the rock.

I edge my body sideways to slide through the next passage, sandstone smooth on my hands. When I come into a yawning space, the canyon walls weaving overhead, I see a friend of mine standing in the middle. The sandy ground beneath him is as flat as a stage. He uses his entire body to describe to me the passage of water through here. His hands reach into the air. He is telling me about a fast, tight corkscrew 120 feet deep, how water acts like a lathe against every surface. He describes a single rock's passage in a flood. It would be hurled through like an electrified pinball. Around and around and around.

"Think about being a person inside of this," he says. "There is no way out."

I walk around him, examining his giant corkscrew flood. The rock walls mirror the path of water. I can see every turn it would take, a monstrous whirlpool sucking from the ceiling to the floor, carving out a passage as smooth and curved as the bowl of a spoon.

I look at him and say, "Did you know that one person survived a flood in here?"

I look back up to the corkscrew, continuing to walk around him, tracing the flood with my eyes. When I come around to his face again, I ask, "What does it mean that somebody was shot from the flood, just cannonballed right out of the canyon alive?"

He doesn't have an answer for that. Was it a fortuitous act or some random pulse in the flood? I don't have an answer either. The mechanisms of water are unbearably complex. A tension is created between the resistance of stone and the erosional power of moving water. This shape that remains — a long, narrow mansion full of dark walkways and parlors — is a geomorphological search for resolution.

I am here seeking resolution as well. I struggle to find a balance between darkness and hope. I can't find the sharp line that I want between the two, not in this canyon. Everything in here is circular, hard to define, with no explicit angles. Severity, elegance, terror, and beauty are inseparable in Antelope Canyon. It is hard to make sense of it because I live in a human world where things are labeled either good or bad. That this canyon and its floods are neither does not sit well with this way of thinking.

We are ventriloquists whenever we speak in here. Our voices turn around and come out someplace else. Every time I move a matter of feet, the sound of my speech or my motion changes from closet to concert hall back to closet. Even writing in my notebook, the scratching of my pen echoes in the tight spaces. I imagine that sound follows the same path as water, waves and ripples curling neatly into the alcoves. A shout would be a bursting wave splashing to the rim. But no one shouts. The canyon urges us to move quietly. I continue to walk, thinking of the *good* and *bad* that we use as labels for everything. Is it good because it is beautiful, then bad because people have died here? We are such simple creatures, I think.

My hands sweep slowly against the walls, opposite sides easily touched at the same time. Even the ancient cross-bedding of the sandstone, the gentle lines left from the rock's origin, are swirled into the shapes. They look like the warp and weft of a loomed textile. I walk into a room where flowers have been left on top of a rock pile at the back of a dimly obscured, ear-shaped chamber. Above the flowers are two names carved almost illegibly into the wall. The names will be taken out by the next flood. I recognize them. These are names of two of the people who

died here, Chee Chin Yang and Thierry Castell. It is strange to hear people speaking out loud in this memorial room — or in this canyon at all. There is a bit of general laughter, a half-posed photo taken. I remember that the people who last died here had cameras with them. They were equally enchanted as they walked through.

To die here, I think, would be like dying in the throat of a black hole in space. Every physical law is brought down to its most principle form. Sound and water and stone and light are the same, equally reshaped in the search for resolution. These people's bodies were stolen into a perfect place. I cannot speak for them or for their surviving families and friends. But I can ask for myself. Would this be the perfect place to die? It would be a swift and difficult death, I know that. Even ghosts are scoured clean from this place. I try to shake the thought from my head, because I remember that children were left behind, their parents killed here where I am standing. I know details about the dead, jewelry that they wore, hobbies, friendships. I spoke with people who pulled the bodies free of the chaotic muck left behind, and I saw the distracted pain of their faces. I know a backcountry ranger who will not come here because friends of hers pulled bodies out and their stories left her too uneasy.

I imagine that they died like this, like us walking through today. Just down here traveling, living life, aghast at the beauty. Each thinking separate thoughts when suddenly, all have the same question: What is that rumbling sound? Then, oblivion.

One of the people with me here is from Australia. He is a world traveler. Running his hand across one of the walls, feeling the pecks and divots left by flood rocks, he tells me that it reminds him of European cities. "Many of the buildings are pocked by bullets and shrapnel from the wars," he says. "All of these marks left in the walls feel like war scars."

We each move up to the wall and caress the holes. "You can feel each rock," I say. "Like here," my finger swiping into a long scratch. "It was a fist-sized rock carried down by a flood."

One woman takes a closer look. "Or a belt buckle," she suggests.

A man glances at her. "You can't say that. That's bad juju."

No part of the bedrock is broken in here. There is hardly a single jagged line. There are no cracks or crumbles or fractures from stress. Each failure in natural, geologic engineering has been washed away by floods. I think of bridge architects and their trussed arches and cantilevers. Could they have built this if an artist couldn't? Could they have suspended these great sculptures of sandstone over our heads with no risk of their falling?

There is a bright place ahead of me. It looks like a blinding spotlight shining against the floor. I walk to it. The walls around glow in blushing light. This is the only place where sunlight comes directly through, hitting the floor. It is the shape of a dagger, so bright I cannot look straight into it. I stretch my hand out. A stark shadow breaks the ground. I turn my hand in the light, studying it, feeling the pulse of warmth.

I wonder, is this what they were thinking before they died? I open my hand so sunlight lands in my palm. My hand looks like it is burning white hot. Were they immersed in the strange beauty of this canyon, in its quirks and miracles, a hand held into a sliver of sunlight, when they heard the sound of a flood moving through like a locomotive? Did they know what it was? When they saw it, did they have any idea that it could be true?

AUGUST 12

The thunderstorm first boils into southern Nevada. Balls of hail 2 inches wide blanket Las Vegas. Then the water comes, flooding the streets. Cars are thrown into each other like reckless barges, scraping sideways along medians. Tropicana Avenue becomes a river 50 feet wide. In the middle of this avenue, a fire truck drives in, acting as a dam to protect a stranded car. A ladder is extended onto the car's roof, and a fireman climbs out, smashes in the windshield, and hauls two people back to the truck. On another street elsewhere in the city, a man sees water rising around his parked truck, so he goes out to move it. As soon as he creeps around to the door, the water buckles his knees. He sweeps beneath his truck and drowns.

Within only an hour, the storm abandons Las Vegas. It rises and dissipates, its singular thunderhead spreading out until even the lightning ceases. It slowly continues to the northeast into Utah, drifting across radar screens, recognizable as nothing but a faint veil of moisture. Seen from an orbiting satellite, desert thunderstorms do not have the deeply coiled grandeur of storms like those taking the entire Eastern Seaboard or those swallowing Louisiana. Infrared images show them as dots of lava, undulations dwarfed in the emptiness of otherwise cloudless skies. What they lack in visual potency from space, they make up for in impact at the surface. Barometric nets look like black holes, with pressure gradients sinking all the way to the ground, sweeping up thousand-foot dust devils. Each cell is disturbingly confined, like a defensive animal shoved into a corner.

This storm that left Las Vegas wanders across southern Utah, taking nearly 24 hours in its journey. On the radar image of the continent, the storm's far southern tip coalesces into only a green pinprick on the Utah-Arizona state line just past the Grand Canyon. Around 3 o'clock in the afternoon, it shows as a bright, roving speck. No other storms accompany it. This dot arrives on the radar screen about the same time as 12 travelers reach northeast Arizona. They have come to see this deep incision in the swells of sandstone called Antelope Canyon. A photographer's dream.

Ella Young, that day's ticket-taker for entry into Antelope, orders the group out of the canyon as the edge of the storm passes over. It is not raining here, but waves of downward clouds can be seen striking the desert all around. They tromp up the ladders to wait 30 minutes, taking shelter under the covered concession stand. They are mostly young, in their 20s and 30s: seven from France, two from the United States, one from Great Britain, and another from Sweden. Five are here with the 12th person, an American tour guide named Pancho Quintana, 28 years old, muscular, 5-feet-8. Quintana works for a British company that caters to young European travelers. They all want back into the canyon to make the most of the last chance of the day for photographs. The storm crawls east, almost out of sight. Young hesitantly gives them the okay.

About 20 miles away, lightning rakes the ground. The thunderstorm ascends the Kaibito Plateau, losing structural stability as it lifts another 2,300 feet. It crosses through cooler layers of atmosphere, forcing water out of its dark vapor. Over a place called Many Ghosts Hill, it becomes a cloudburst, dumping its rain. The flood begins there.

Within Antelope, photos are taken, the curve of sandstone admired. The place is entirely overhung, impossible to climb. For the amazement of the sensation, people touch both walls at once, leaning their heads back to inhale this confined hugeness. They look for the sky. What little of it they can see is completely clear of clouds. They stand in small circles of tilted sunlight. Walking slowly in the canyon's half light, they return to the ladders that will take them to the rim. Just behind a young man from France, Quintana reaches the top of the first ladder. A Swedish man and English woman, both in their early 20s, beckon him down to

take their picture, so he climbs 80 feet back to the canyon floor. They pose. Quintana snaps a shot.

They all stop when they hear it. They do not breathe at the crescendo, as the ground shudders like hoof beats. The moment is as still from thought as possible. A blunt mass of dark water surges into view. It splits around the ladders above them. Streams of water and foam cut through the metal steps into the air. Tangled inside this water is the Frenchman, struggling to breathe, to get out. His face spears through the water, screaming. Bowled over, he tries to keep his ground. He can't. The vision is terrifying. They watch him as he is thrown unwittingly toward them.

So huge and fast, the vision needles straight into their stomachs. No one plans on dying this way, so suddenly. They run. But downcanyon holds no escape for them. Only more darkness. Deeper falls. The water at the front of the flood winds up their calves. This first water is thick with objects, rumbling as it carries large stones. And behind that, it carries boulders.

The flood cuts behind their knees, flipping them over. Quintana grabs the two that he photographed and shoves them against the wall. They press all over each other, wedging against a curve in the rock. Faces against shoulder blades against arms. There is not a second of delusion. The water is rising. They will not live. The curve that is their shelter was formed by water, left from where it is most turbulent. It is not a good place to hide. It is the only place they have. Quintana digs his fingers into someone's flesh, trying to hold on. To save them. To save himself. The Frenchman hits them, grabbing wildly as he washes past. The two Quintana holds rip away.

For a second he sees their struggles. Parts of their flexing bodies show through the sand and mud. The swift material lifts above his head, and he loses his grip on the wall.

Everyone is on their own now. No one can help anyone. Quintana does the right things. He points his feet downstream, keeps his butt and legs up, the way you are taught if thrown from a raft. His arms strap around his head. The water is full of rocks, boulders. They do not ride the floor. Rather, they sail. If you got your head under there, your spine would be jerked in half. But the right things are irrelevant in here. Everything is up to the flood. His body is pummeled. His clothes are torn free. Boots, socks, underwear. Objects beat against his bones, sanding off his flesh. He holds his breath for so long, with so many rocks striking his abdomen, that his stomach lining rips open. Mud packs under his eyelids, and he is blinded.

Three times he feels something solid, part of the wall. Three times his grasp is sheared free. He is lifted on a crest and scraped into a rock ledge. Now he gets his fingernails into something. He hauls himself to a higher exposed ledge, gasping. Mud drools from his lungs, and he pukes it out. Breathing is painful. He doesn't know where he is or how he landed here. He can hear water thundering all around him, but he can't see through the mud jammed under his eyelids. There is no way he can tell if he is safe or if he is about to be swept away. He is in a tunnel of unbearable noise.

The flood keeps running past him. The canyon swallows the water down with a gutteral roar. Deep, percussive sounds come. And the boulders. They are moving through, striking along the floor far below the surface of the water. Quintana digs at his eyes, trying to see. He collapses. His memory goes dead.

The next person to come is a state trooper. He finds Quintana on a ledge, his naked body horrifically bruised and raw. A helicopter is called to get him to help. Quintana tries to talk. He is unsure of what happened. Losing consciousness, coming back, vomiting mud, he does not understand why he is alive.

A man from the nearby town of Page arrives. He takes off his own shirt and covers Quintana. To soothe him, to hide the wounds. To do something, anything. The man from Page, a maintenance man, Little League coach, and father, looks over the edge. Far into the canyon the flood is 20 feet deep, subsiding already. The current makes him think of miracles and of God and of how there is simply no way anyone could survive.

That night the first body is found. A woman. She had been washed 5½ miles down waterfalls, around boulders, wracked through 2-foot-wide causeways, then blown 100 yards up *a side canyon. It is days before anyone else is found.*

The next day, blame is announced through national newspapers and television coverage. Cameras on tripods are lined along the canyon rim, footage sent back in time for evening news. The ticket taker, Ella Young, is the first to feel outside pressure. She is accused of letting people into Antelope under dangerous circumstances. The blame then turns to the only survivor, Pancho Quintana, and the company that hired him. But Quintana was employed only as a general tour guide. His job description involved mostly logistics and van-driving, making sure food and lodging is arranged, telling engaging stories in the evenings. Bringing clients to Antelope Canyon was one stop of many in a state-to-state tour. He could have predicted this flood as accurately as predicting an earthquake. If he had been intimate with deserts and storms, he might be expected to think twice before coming in as a thunderhead passed by. But he was a low-paid chaperon. He had no clear reason to hold his clients back. A summer day will see over a hundred tourists walking down Antelope Canyon. This place is a public spectacle, giving it a false veil of safety. Quintana is not the one to blame. Nor is Ella Young.

Andrea Lankford, called in from her post as a ranger at Grand Canyon National Park, searches the stagnant water in coming days. Like her companions, she wears a wet suit and is up to her shoulders in sludge. It is like liquid peat bog, covered with a rug of floating juniper scales and their hard, bluish berries. The work is slow, sorting by hand through dead frogs, dead bottom-feeder fish, dead rodents, cow dung, uprooted sagebrush — the ejecta of a flood left unfinished in the backwash of an artificial reservoir called Lake Powell, which is at the end of Antelope

Canyon. The rotten smell of death is overwhelming. A cigar prods the air from her mouth, perfuming the scent of death so that she can breathe. Her arms stretch forward, feeling through the debris for bodies. She shoves branches out of her path.

Every hour or so Lankford and the other searchers swim back to a waiting house boat that motors them into clear reservoir water. There they dive to clean themselves. Lankford has pulled numerous bodies out

of complicated areas, but nothing like this. In places she struggles to keep her face out of the soup. Hepatitis shots are administered when they come out.

Two days after the flood, the body of an American man born in Malaysia is found in the debris field. The next is a 20-year-old woman from France, found only a matter of inches away from a friend of hers, another young French woman. Next comes a 24-year-old English woman identified by a handmade silver ring on the middle finger of her right hand, followed by an American photographer, a 32-year-old French woman, and a 40-year-old French mother whose two daughters had been found alone and terrified in a Page motel two days earlier.

The debris field produces seven bodies, all within 25 feet of each other, thrown against the west wall. There is no clear reason as to why they are so well ordered here while the first one was spun up a higher side canyon miles away. Lankford swims, pushing bodies ahead of her, maneuvering them toward the house boat. Each body is naked. Autopsies will show drowning as the cause of death. One person clearly has a broken neck and broken arm. One searcher comments that they look as if they had been through a blender. What leaves Lankford uneasy is a man wearing only a belt with an empty camera bag. As if the water chose one thing and not the other. This she can't figure out. Boulders are moved, disintegrated. Boots and jewelry are torn free. Then she finds a dead woman with a sports bra pulled snug.

Another body, the father of the two girls stranded in Page, is released

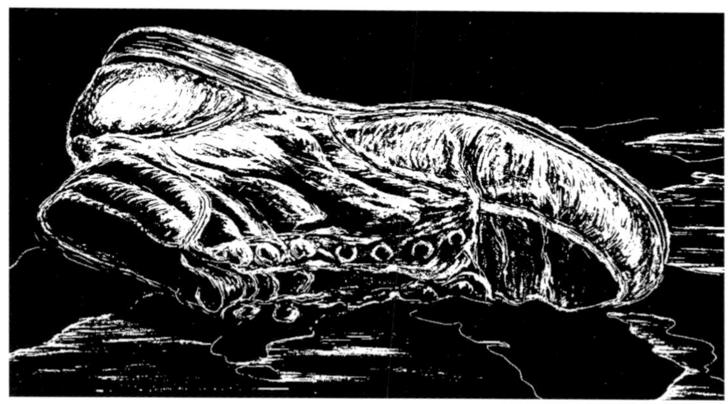

by Lake Powell on August 17, a Sunday. The final two bodies are never found, probably buried deep among the sunken boulders. Meanwhile, a number of Navajo tribal members hold a quiet, mandatory ceremony to clear the place of death.

PHANTOM CANYON, GRAND CANYON

There is a hole where the water sings. The hole is a canyon that clamps down on itself. The place is called Phantom, one of the many canyons inside the Grand Canyon. A small creek wanders inside, its voice echoing in its descent.

It is early evening when I reach the hole, hiking for a couple days from the south, across a place called Utah Flats. I pull out my sleeping bag and start dinner cooking on a small stove.

Behind me, the land is a vast opening of cliffs and steep chasms, classic of the Grand Canyon's interior. Sunset still holds the highest cliffs. Ahead of me is this plunging hole where bedrock is worn smooth. It stoops out of view. There are no plants in there, no customary boulders or small rocks. No broken cottonwood trees. No sand. No dirt. When my meal of rice and beans is ready, I walk with the pan in a gloved hand. Reaching in with a spoon, eating distractedly, I step around the edge of this hole. It is like walking the rim of a bowl clean as stainless steel. A huge boulder is jammed into a nick at the upstream end, turned smooth as ice by the polishing force of floods. Water of Phantom Creek strains into this place, running down a smoothed ladle of stone into a dusky canyon. The sound is opulent. Long tails of creek water spatter and gurgle. I crouch there on the rim, taking another bite. The water is a meditation, a sweet sound.

As the last light slips out and the stars come, I am still crouching there with this crystalline timbre of running water. This is why people place miniature, burbling fountains on their desks at work, why they linger beside rivers. The libretto tones of water settle the electrical storm of the mind. This little creek is alert, though, not sleepy. Every now and then it perks with a sudden high pitch. I've listened to floods, as well as these trickles of water. The voice is different, but it is still water song. It is still baritone and shrill at once.

The next morning, I gather a day's worth of gear and walk upstream to follow the course of the most recent flood, a big September deluge from a month ago. By tracking the path of rubble, I will be able to find the source.

Entire groves of thin willows are bent to the ground, their leaves matted with mud and roots from upstream. The largest of the surviving willows are 17 inches in diameter. Anything larger did not bend in the flood. It broke. The big willows are gone.

Only the established cottonwood trees survived. The young ones were yanked out, their entire root balls twisted from the ground. If they weren't dug out by the flood, they were severed, leaving broken stumps standing around like gravestones, some cocked into the direction of the flow, ragged tops decorated with hanging wreckage. Eight-foot-high bridges of broken cottonwood trunks stand locked together, the arms of branches linked. Logjams of 30 full-grown trees thrust into each other. Amidst the debris I find the skinned leg of a fox. Claws and articulated toe bones are held in place by scrappy tendons. I sit on my haunches and lift the remains with my right hand. I rotate it. The four darkened toe pads are still in place.

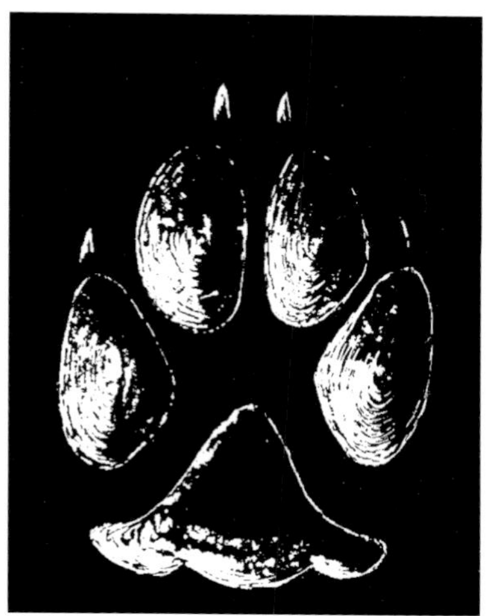

Tracks of a trotting coyote show in the aftermath mud nearby. It came through sniffing at the fresh green snap of willows. Surrounded by upended trees and toppled boulders, the small tracks seem too individual, too cognizant, heading upstream instead of downstream. In view of the flood damage, they are as trivial as bystanders.

Where Phantom Canyon splits into two major feeder canyons, it is obvious that the flood came from the northeast. The western continuation of Phantom Canyon looks untouched, its trees still standing. Haunted Canyon, the northern addition, is heaped with debris. Roots swim to the surface of log piles. I turn up Haunted and follow it.

I had made acquaintance with the storm that sent down this recent flood. At the time, I was in a canyon not far to the west of Phantom and

Haunted when one of the largest floods I had ever witnessed came through. It grew from beneath a thunderhead after only two minutes of rain, sending boulders and entire trees through. I watched from a ledge, pinning my body against the cliff wall behind me.

A week later, I hiked to the Colorado River, the exit point for this flood. A raft group happened by in the evening, and we camped together. Three of the boatmen along were Pat Phillips, Bret Stark, and a man called Okie. They each had been parked at Havasu Canyon the month before when their boats were blown end over end by a flood. We spent hours sharing stories.

When I mentioned seeing a large flood just a week ago, they all asked questions, curious about its size and the force. Stark asked if I was going to be walking along the river from here. I told him I hadn't decided which way I'd go yet, but following the river was one of my thoughts.

"Why do you ask?"

"Well, if you're down here," he said, "keep your eye out. Phantom Canyon flooded, and they haven't found one of the bodies yet. Sounds like it'll show up in the river somewhere."

"A week ago?" I asked.

"Seven days," he said. "Probably the same storm system that flooded you. Friends of ours found one body near Tapeats Creek, and they tied her to shore so she wouldn't float away."

There was quiet for a bit. I looked out to the river. I had escaped the last storm so easily, climbing up to a ledge, my face finger-painted with flood mud, muscles shaking. To know that it killed people nearby did not change the water in my mind, but immediately I sensed my own breathing and the easy beating of my heart.

I looked back at Stark and asked, "So if I see a body floating down the river, you're thinking I can somehow grab it?"

He gave me a grim smile. "No. I guess you just have to watch it go by."

I decided not to follow the river. I did not want to stand helplessly, seeing a dead man come and go.

Traveling up Haunted Canyon for the next few hours, I worked among the gaunt, broken remains of September's flood. I ducked through the locked trunks of trees and ran my hands into gaping cavities in the ground where boulders were once planted. The eagerness of the flood had been replaced by stillness.

Everything is waiting for the next thrust of motion. The violence is redeemed by today's patience and placidity.

There is one place where cottonwood trees have been left in the form of a jungle gym dome. Out from under this dome comes a chant of canyon tree frogs. Their voices are each of a different tone, hard to

tell how many, maybe 15 or 20. As if invited into a ceremonial hut, I crawl beneath the canopy into an open space, skirting over boulders. In the middle, the creek has pooled behind a dam of rock and wood. Bright purple flowers of western redbud trees float across the surface like Hawaiian leis. The edges of the pool are lined with silver-gray canyon treefrogs, each the size of a matchbook. They swell and collapse as they call, membranes around their throats pulsing outward.

The voices are percussion instruments, a mix of ratchets and marimbas. I listen to one, then another, each voice separated by octaves and half-steps. Put together, they produce a riveting drone. I crawl in closer. A few of the frogs shift uncomfortably. Others freeze. The noise goes on. They are basking in these new niches and enclaves left by the flood. For them, the flood is a blessing. Certainly, many were lost. But even that is a blessing, dissolving the glut of competition. I move forward just another inch. Too much, though. Frogs suddenly go catapulting every direction, slapping into the water. Their pale bodies plummet to the bottom, scooting beneath drowned leaves and branches. The place is suddenly quiet except for the trickle of water. Shadows drop through the flood debris over my head. Branches are interlocked like antlers. The flood isn't gone. I feel it around me. The big water is gone, yes. But everything else is still here, every cataract and mood of the flood, every remnant of scale.

In the evening, I return and again fix my meal and carry it to the edge of the hole. Hours later I am still crouching, the canyon dark. There is not a single frog voice down there. It is clean. I stand and walk slowly around the deep chute. I squint to see down in the darkness. Is this a tomb, or is it the eye of a needle? This canyon will continue ushering floods for hundreds of thousands, even millions, of years. Undoubtedly, other people will die here. To call it a tomb, though, would be arrogant. This canyon pre-dates the human species. Our lives here are as fleeting as the floods themselves.

The loss of life seems far away. Death is at the bottom of a hole that has no end as far as I can see, and I am at the top peering in. Even considering my experiences with floods, it is difficult for me to recapture the horror that must have been felt when people were in the pit of Phantom Canyon. The petrifying roar of trees, boulders, and water compressed into an alleyway of rock seems unattainable right now. All I hear is the constant language of babbling stream water.

SEPTEMBER 11

The storm enters the Grand Canyon at a high butte called The Dragon. It breaks apart, sending itself out, lighting striking the points of rock that stand from of the Canyon like heaved idols. The storm overtakes a place called Shiva Temple, wrapping into an amphitheater canyon known as the Buddha Cloister. All of the names in this part of the Grand Canyon are theatrical. The landscape matches the names. Canyons engulf each other. On the opposite side of the Grand Canyon from Shiva Temple is a point called Mohave. The wind comes strong here, pushing away from the center of the storm. It is not raining on Mohave Point yet. A young German tourist stands on the farthest edge, watching the convulsions of clouds, how they fold into each other like tremendous, dark blankets. The force of the storm is palpable and mesmerizing. He sees rain in the distance. It comes in violet-colored sheets, swallowing the North Rim 14 miles across from him. The air smells rich with water. He has to spread his legs to stand against the wind. The ground vibrates. His skin prickles.

What he never sees is the stroke of lightning. It reaches clear across the Grand Canyon like an arm outstretched where there had been no arm before. It comes so fast that there is not even a flash registered in his eyes. The bolt of lightning strikes him directly, blowing him back from the edge. He lands on the ground, his body hitting like a sack of oranges. A woman standing behind him is also blown over, taking burns across her body.

When rescuers arrive, they find tourists administering CPR to the man. His heart is still beating, although his unconscious body shivers and charges from respiratory arrest. The woman is conscious. She has first- and second-degree burns. Attention is focused on the man. They hold a mask around his nose and mouth, forcing pure oxygen into his lungs. The rhythm of his breath slowly returns as they work. He will live.

Ken Phillips, the head of search and rescue for the Grand Canyon, is at the scene, lifting the man into a gurney. A tone comes across the radio on his hip. He reaches back and turns up the volume. Flash flood, the voice says. Phantom Creek. He looks up from the edge of Mohave Point. His eyes track across the Grand Canyon. On the other side from him, below the temples and spires, is Phantom Canyon. It is incised so deeply than none of it can be seen. Storms are plunging into it from the

rims, arms of murky clouds reaching into every canyon that leads to Phantom. It looks as if an preposterously huge creature is sliding in. His first thought: Is anybody out there?

Indeed, there are people out there. A woman, her brother, and her husband. With backpacks they had walked down to the popular Bright Angel Campground in the floor of the Grand Canyon. The couple, 39 and 40 years old, came on vacation from New Orleans for four days of foot travel through the canyons. The woman is a nurse practitioner and president of a hospice. Her husband is a police officer. The younger brother, studying to be a nurse practitioner, came from Chicago. He is in his mid-30s. They had set camp, spending their first night beneath stars and a clear sky.

On this, their second day inside the Grand Canyon, they get a late start, walking a northward trail until reaching the confluence of Bright Angel Creek and the narrow hall of Phantom Canyon. Phantom has a dark gravity to it that Bright Angel does not. Its black walls cut immediately out of view. It is as enticing as the devil peeking around a corner. Even with storms bearing down from the north, the sky directly overhead is fairly clear, sputtering out bits of rain now and then. Often the storms won't come this low, sizzled away by the heat of the desert. Several thousand feet above the three of them, 2 inches of rainfall would be recorded for this day, while down here the gauges show barely 1/20 of an inch.

They leave the trail and start up this inviting canyon whose head begins at 8,000 feet where 2 inches of rain are now falling. Moving through clear, shallow water, a year-round creek sent from the North Rim, they splash up onto boulders and wade through crystalline pools. The flashing, orchestral tones of water draw them farther up the canyon.

It would be paradise, a muscle-relaxing, linen-clean scene for a Maxfield Parrish painting, except for the depth and claustrophobic squeeze of the canyon, except for the darkening of its stone, how shadows cast across each other. There is always a bit of fear in these canyons. The travelers drown it out as best they can. The youngest of the three goes ahead until reaching the glint of a clear waterfall. Sunlight breaks through clouds, leading down into the canyon. It is going to be a fine

day, he thinks. Soon they will all three be here in the sun, mesmerized by the sweet spray of this waterfall.

He returns to the other two, offering a hand so that his sister can cross the boulders without getting too wet. He says that there is a waterfall up ahead. Beautiful. His hand goes out. He hears a deep-throated roar from the canyon behind him. At that moment his sister's eyes dart upstream, held suddenly still. A word forms on her lips. Then she shouts it, "Water! WATER!"

He wheels around. Cresting over the top of the falls is something unimaginable. Like a wall of rust-red lava, a flash flood thunders down, consuming the entire waterfall. The space it occupies, the sound, the speed, the color, these are all impossible. A moment before was the sweet chime of a waterfall. Now they have no more than 15 seconds.

His eyes shoot downstream. The first instinct. Run. *At a full sprint he could reach a clearing 50 feet away, a place where he could scramble to safety. But if he runs, what of his sister and brother-in-law? He glances quickly at the two of them, and their eyes are frozen. They seem no longer connected to their bodies. They are not going to run. In fact, if he doesn't grab them out of their sudden stupor, they will be bowled end over end, no chance of survival. He is the one with outdoors experience. He knows that one should not freeze, that the deepest instinct, the one that says* MOVE, *is the only one to follow now. But if he leaves them here, they will die.*

Ten seconds now. He yards back on his sister's arm, shouting for her to move, to follow him. If they won't run, they need to at least find protection. Eight seconds. There is a boulder nearby, about 8 feet tall, leaning against the canyon wall. He shouts again. Get behind that boulder! *Their eyes turn to him as if just out of a dream, not yet awake. They almost float as they move, drifting without gravity. Seven seconds. He yells again, dragging them along. Six seconds.*

They each crowd into the space, backing up to the boulder. Arms lock into arms, seeking protection. Three seconds. The sound rises like some godless creature. The young brother thinks, in that final moment, of dinosaurs. This, he thinks, is what it must have been like to have a Tyrannosaurus rex *coming down on top of you. No way out. The thing is huge and angry. It has sabers for teeth.*

One second.

"Please, God," he says. "Please."

The boulder shudders at the impact. It feels as if it might topple on them, 40 tons of rock turning over in the wall of a flood. But it does not come down. Like a huge ocean wave cresting with white caps, the flood wall passes. Water shoots through gaps behind the boulder. The slurry pounds over the top, twisting around on them. Currents immediately reel up their bodies chest-deep, pulling them apart. The boulder does nothing. There is no protection. The flood is everywhere.

He shouts instructions:

"We're going to get swept away! Keep your legs pointed downstream! Keep on your backs!"

But the other two do not hear him. Their eyes glaze in such a deep horror that their selves are gone, to who knows where. Somewhere safe and far away. He shouts again as the red water lifts, pulling him out from behind the boulder. He can barely get the words out now, Save yourselves, *when the water has him. It sucks him into the flow. He tries to follow his own advice: Point his feet downstream to fend off objects. Float on his back so that his head can stay in the air.*

None of this happens. He is taken straight to the bottom, his body no longer his own. His legs yank down, then behind him, rolling him over and over. The sound of the flood thrums underwater, the garble of furious air bubbles, barrels of air taken down with him. The canyon wall comes. He feels it. His body collides with it, rolling violently along its surface. Then something else. It is a boulder. A moving boulder. It rides up into his chest and he passes beneath it as if under a steam roller. Then the wall again.

Where is the air? He has not breathed for some time. His head surges out, and he catches a mouthful, breathing in mud and water and enough oxygen to keep him alive for a little longer. As he comes back down, a broken cottonwood tree thrusts into the right side of his head, sending him deeper.

He knows he is a good swimmer. He has performed well in triathalons in the past. There must be some way. But no matter how much force he commands of his body, he cannot muscle his way to control. He feels exhaustion setting in. The need for air.

Then he is out. A stray current sends him straight up, firing him like a missile. He is clear of the flood, completely above it. Flying. He takes a full breath. He can see the canyon walls around him. Cottonwood trees recoiling against the water. The sky. Freedom. But he sees all this for only that second. He falls from the air. Instantly he is down. He hits the floor of the canyon. There is gravel down here. The rocks are smaller, grating along the back of his head. He knows he is at the bottom.

By now the flood has carried him half a mile. He has taken only three breaths in this span. At the bottom he feels the ache. He must breathe. Soon his reflexes will take over for him. He cannot stop the urge to breathe. He will drown. Once he knows this, the flood pulling at his appendages, knotting them around each other because he has no resistance, he lets go. Death will come quickly, he thinks. And it is not so bad. He is a religious man. He has made his peace.

We fight so hard to survive. But to die takes this last, greatest strength. There is no terror now. He waits for it to come, the final gasp that will fill his lungs. He quietly ignores the pain and panic of his body.

Then he thinks of his wife. The pain and panic she will feel. His right hand hits something solid. It is not one of the many moving boulders. This one stays put. He catches a finger hold just as his body swings into an eddy behind the boulder. The water is shallow here. He figures he must be off to the side of the flood. He is face down. When he lifts his head, he finds air. He pulls it in, then coughs out red mud, his lungs seizing on him. A light current carries him along the shore of Bright

Angel Creek. He has come into a calm area, but hardly has the strength to clutch the young cottonwood trees going by, the shoots and elastic saplings. He finally gets a hold of one and pulls himself free.

He does not know what has happened. How can he know? Not more than a minute ago, he was reaching out to help his sister. He had been aroused by a sense of awe, the canyon huge around him, the beauty of a waterfall. Now here, suddenly, he slops his way into shallow mud. Where is his sister? She was in his hands moments ago. And his brother-in-law, there beside him?

The clear, tiny creek is gone. Now a tumultuous street of red water and mud rumbles through. Boulders detonate deep beneath. Objects become snared in rafts of debris, settling out in eddies as the flood moves down Bright Angel Creek, then on to the Colorado River.

Downstream from him, a torn piece of a blue waist pack snags against the shoreline. Just upstream is a blue sock and the broken frame of a pair of sunglasses. Much farther downstream is another blue sock, a pair of boxers, a yellow sandal, a white bandanna. The flood has rifled their belongings. It has searched their pockets, their gear, pulled their clothes off. Everything is left strewn and torn apart.

He is one of the pieces of debris. The silt had acted like sandpaper on his eyeballs. Now everything he sees is backlit by a halo. He crawls from the water to dry ground. He is bleeding. Any part of his body that stands out — ankles, shins, backbone, elbows, forehead, and ears — is missing skin. The flood had tried to turn him into something else.

When he finds the strength, he stands. He knows that he is the sole survivor. His sister and brother-in-law are gone. He looks up into the hazy-bright sky through hundreds of scratches on his corneas. He is a Christian. He believes in God. And this God, he thinks, where was he?

"Where were you?" *he demands. Then he throws his fists, tears coming out red with mud.* "HOW COULD YOU DO THIS?" *Mud streams down his face.*

He begins to run, fumbles, almost falls, then runs faster. As he runs, he shouts at this God, hurling insults and incensed questions. He does not understand how this could happen. In the time of greatest need,

God did nothing for them. Not for his sister, not for his brother-in-law. And what was this? Allowing him to live. Punishment? He screams at the sky. Furious. Out of control. He heaves his arms. He throws rocks, sticks. Over and over, WHAT HAVE YOU DONE?

After 20 minutes, he has no more energy to confront the heavens. He crumples on the ground. His first clear thought comes into his head. Not since he offered a hand to his sister, telling her of the beautiful waterfall just ahead, had his mind functioned in any customary way. He thinks that he should get up. He should find help.

Next, he is in a room. A helicopter had transported him to the South Rim only an hour after the flood. He knows he is the survivor. The only one. They do not need to tell him this. A desk is positioned strategically between him and a law enforcement official arranging paperwork. The survivor's hair is matted with mud. Streaks of blood and abrasions cross his arms, chest, and face. The more impressive wounds have been cleaned and bandaged. He does not fidget or look about the room. His vision is still cloudy. It has been, at the most, two hours since he was saved by the boulder and the eddy. Two hours since they died. He doesn't have much sense of time.

The officer, wearing a tie and a badge, looks up at him, studying the pale, shocked complexion, the ghastly eyes. He has seen this too many times. A disaster, people dead, a bewildered survivor. He is almost angry that this has happened and at the same time unbearably saddened that he can do nothing and that he finds himself here in this role. He cannot shout or cry or run away. Strangers have died, he thinks. He controls his emotions, quieting himself so that he can gather the needed information — a technique common among those who must often deal with death. He says that he has a few questions. The survivor nods for him to go ahead.

"Whose idea was it to come here?"

"Mine," he answers, his voice flat, the only voice he can offer.

"Had you been here before?"

"Yes."

"And the other two had never been backpacking before?"

"Correct."

"You were the trip leader?"

"Yes."

"Did you know about flash flood dangers?"

"Yes."

"How did you know?"

"People were killed in a canyon in Arizona. A couple weeks ago. I heard about it."

"Did you think that there was danger in this canyon?"

"I thought there could be danger, yes."

"Why did you go?"

The survivor pauses. His breathing is shallow. The event plays through his head with high volume. He can't turn it off. Did he kill them, he wonders. Had he performed some terrible act? Or was it strictly the result of a flood? Was he an ordinary man thrown into an extraordinary circumstance, or was he a killer? He feels swollen muscles, a rash of sound, boulders crashing into each other like freeway impacts. But the room is quiet, fluorescent lights humming. He hears the crisp turn of a page under the officer's fingers.

"I don't know," he says.

"You don't know?"

The survivor swallows. "We were hiking," he finally answers.

"Hiking?"

"Yes."

"But in that narrow canyon, when a flash flood was coming, you must have had some idea."

"I thought it could happen. Yes."

"And you still went into the canyon. You knew you were putting lives at risk?"

"Yes. Am I in trouble?"

"I don't know. That's what I'm here to figure out. Why did you go into that canyon?"

"We were hiking."

The officer takes a heavy inward breath, then lets it out. He draws his pen over the answers he has written down. "You were the trip leader," he recites. "You knew about flash floods. You had been here before."

"It was sunny," the survivor says, partly in his own defense.

"Sunny?"

"Seventy-five percent clear, I think."

"But you knew a storm was near."

"Yes. I knew."

Again, the hard breath of the officer. He has seen this before. So many times. Foolish people dying, getting people that they love killed. For what? To go hiking? Drownings, rockslides, falls. He is even more inwardly angry now. He carefully holds down his emotions, the scientific, professional control he must maintain.

The evidence leads to only one place. The survivor sits and breathes into the pit of this realization. He had killed his sister and brother-in-law. He would someday, years away from this room, come to the conclusion that he is not a murderer, but for this moment he is sure that he is. All of his interior, emotional defenses have failed in this line of questions. He is finally broken.

The air stands taut between the two of them, a tightwire strung between human ignorance and the relentless happenstance of nature. Both the officer and the survivor struggle quietly with this division, while thousands of feet below them, miles away, the last of the floodwater trickles lightly from Phantom Canyon.

[epilogue]

Sitting in the sun at the bottom of a canyon, I clutch a handful of notes.

Earlier, a flood had come through, striking into the heart of the Grand Canyon. The sixth of seven floods I have seen this September, it was one of those explosive beasts emerging from a quick thunderhead. The sky looked as if it might have opened and swallowed the earth.

I had run through its first waters, sprinting into the lower, narrow canyon for a view as the slurry rose up my legs, finally sending me scrambling for safety. I had listened to the drumbeats of boulders beneath the humbling waves.

The notes I took record quick, minimal measurements. The paper now is wrinkled by sun-dried water. With my fingernail I scratch mud off some of the figures.

The floods that came in 1997, I think of them often.

Why do I survive situations in which others die? Perhaps the answer is that I am looking for floods, and they are not. As I hike, my eyes constantly scan for escape exits. Before I need to, I make decisions — whether I would run down canyon if a flood comes, or up into the face of the flood, hoping to outpace it back to a safe place. I see floods in the canyon walls and the boulders, in snags of debris. When I'm in the floor of a canyon, I know at every moment that I am inside a flood, even when there is no water at all.

Only two hours ago, this canyon upheaved mayhem. Now, there's no sound even as loud as a whisper. No breeze, no clattering of dry leaves, no trickle of water. My riffling through papers makes the loudest intrusion.

With superstitious disquiet, I note that, in the 1997 floods, the names of the places seem sinister, almost prescient of disaster.

The town where the Mexican migrants began their journey, Agua Prieta, means Dark Water. The flood at Antelope Canyon started at Many Ghosts Hill. The Haunted Canyon flood flowed from there into a place called Phantom Canyon. The only person to survive the flood crawled out of the water where it entered Bright Angel Creek. How many ghosts reside at Many Ghosts Hill? Are there 11 more now?

Perhaps the most telling fact to draw from those floods is that only one of the 22 who died in them lived nearby. The others came from places as far away as Sweden and the highlands of Mexico, from New Orleans and England. I imagine most of them could hardly conceive of floods in such a dry land. Perhaps that is why they were caught so much by surprise.

I also think of the social and political aftermath of the floods: the scurry of press conferences and public outcry, the obsessive attempts to affix blame for the deaths, the claims for money to pay for deaths, injuries, and damages.

Immediately after the Antelope Canyon flood, agencies of the federal government and the Navajo Nation held meetings to consider initiating safety precautions and installing warning systems.

For a while, the lower section of Antelope Canyon was closed to visitors, rigged with barbed wire. The canyon would not be reopened until two-way radio communication was established between all guides inside the canyon and an off-site weather official. Rescue nets were placed along the canyon's rim, with the intent of dropping them down the canyon's walls in case of flood. Thus, people on the canyon floor could climb up the nets to safety.

Use of such nets seems to ignore obvious technical difficulties — would the nets survive the tons of boulders and debris crashing through the canyon long enough for visitors to climb them?

The aftermath continued: The National Weather Service offered explanations why a "garden variety" desert storm killed 11 people.

The Bureau of Land Management considered instituting a permit system for travel in all narrow Southwest canyons and talked about forbidding access to the most remote canyons.

Brightly colored warning signs were planted at Antelope Canyon.

Researchers at the University of Arizona announced that they had been working on an early-warning system based on intensive daily forecasts that may have averted the disaster.

A number of officials demanded that electronic monitors be placed in every known canyon to transmit data via satellite to a central command that could rapidly deploy emergency response teams.

The retort to all of this is that the localized thunderstorm over Antelope Canyon on August 12 would not have registered as out of the ordinary on any cautionary system. Rain never even fell in the town of Page, 5 miles away from the flood site. If emergency response teams were notified, by the time they picked up their phones, before they could grab their car keys, the wall of water would have struck.

In the end, I find all of the talk contemptible. Wiring a canyon, any canyon, is such an assuming act as to be treacherous. It will not make the desert safe for those who do not know its ways, but they may think it is safe.

Lawsuits bloomed out of the Antelope Canyon flood. Three French families who lost their children served up a case through a New York celebrity lawyer. The only survivor, the guide whose stomach lining was surgically replaced with an implanted metal mesh, sued. He claimed he did not receive vigorous-enough warnings to stay out of the canyon that day.

Far to the south of Antelope, in the border town of Douglas, some deaths were blamed on a metal grate that had trapped a number of the victims. There were demands to know who gave the okay for installing it. Heads rolled.

Even Mike Moore, the helicopter pilot who flew like a warning flare down Havasu Canyon, had to endure the anger of his supervisor at the Grand Canyon heliport. His audacious flight had violated company policy. Some of his fellow pilots disparagingly called him "cowboy."

After the derailment near Kingman, Amtrak sent a letter to the city of Kingman, giving thanks for the heroic rescue efforts and for the remarkable volunteerism shown by residents who took care of passengers. Amtrak held a barbecue for the town in appreciation. A month later, Amtrak filed a claim asking payment from Kingman, as well as Mojave County and the state of Arizona, to pay claims from injured passengers and property damage.

Blame is a bitter, spiteful thing compared with the fierce honesty of the floods. We want to collect damages in the form of millions of dollars from anyone who made the most trivial of misjudgments. Sometimes we search so hard for cause and culpability that we go blind with a terrible madness. We cannot bear to look the flood in the face.

Even all of my studies appear foolish as I try to frame the flood, to break it down into math. I am looking for accountability in my studies. I am attempting to remove the meanness of flash floods by familiarizing myself with their actions.

This flood that came through earlier today, was it the size of the storm, the length of this drainage, the volume of debris, or the architecture of the canyon? Was it per-minute-precipitation or was it bed gradient?

I would later feed my numbers into a computer, calculating statistical relationships. Diligent as a personal injury lawyer hunting the facts of a case, I am trying to find the meaning that hides inside of floods.

It seems petty that I struggle to find resolution when a flood manifests such raw and indelible beauty. I sometimes wish to throw all of my papers into the passing waters, surrendering my inquiries, accepting the deaths and lives as equal.

Whatever it is that I learn from these potent events, I cannot record it with my pen. It cannot be found in this book.

I sometimes think that, in the perfect Eden, there are no floods. In Utopia, a person never dies fighting beneath muddy waves. Then I am glad to not live in such barren places as these. Floods belong to a fertile and dynamic land. We cannot control elements of danger, magnificence, and prowess in the world. To wish them away or to tear them into survivable pieces is to wish for a less genuine Earth.

I lean over, my hat brim shading the papers in my lap, so that the white glare doesn't hurt my eyes. Other papers lie scattered around my legs. I write numbers with a ballpoint pen.

I stop. There is a sound. It comes clearly from upcanyon. At first it is like static, far away. The sky directly above me is a burning September blue. But I don't look up to the sky. I keep my head in the circle of shade, not moving, so that I can listen to this advancing sound. The pen hangs unused in my right hand.

Becoming more refined, the static sounds like gravel under marching feet. Not an animal. Not wind.

The noise crescendos into a steady rumble. I know exactly what it is, but how is this possible? Another flood? There must be a storm out of sight from here, pouring into the distant head of this canyon. Perhaps it is the same storm from this morning, circling back for another pass. The sound grows, rocks striking each other, the dark splash of water heavy with mud.

I close my eyes for a moment to prepare myself. It is coming. Again.